Contents

44

Law
of
Industrial
Pollution
Control

Andrew Walker, LL.M

Solicitor
Lecturer in Law, University of Aston in Birmingham

Law
of
Industrial
Pollution
Control

George Godwin Limited

The book publishing subsidiary of
The Builder Group

First published in Great Britain 1979 by
George Godwin Limited
The book publishing subsidiary of
The Builder Group
1–3 Pemberton Row, London EC4P 4HL

© Andrew Walker 1979

British Library Cataloguing in Publication Data

Walker, Andrew
 Law of industrial pollution control.
 1. Pollution – Law and legislation –
 Great Britain I. Title
 344'.41 '0463   KD3359

ISBN 0–7114–4205–3

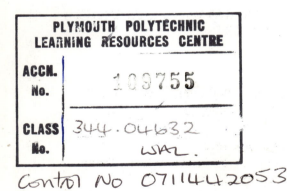
Printed in Great Britain
by Unwin Brothers Limited
The Gresham Press, Old Woking, Surrey

Preface

The purpose of this book is to give an up-to-date statement of the law controlling pollution as it affects the setting up and operation of industrial enterprises. It is intended as a working tool and reference for the plant manager who is responsible for meeting legal constraints and standards while avoiding costly process or operational changes; and equally for the local authority or other responsible officer who must administer law which is to a large extent still in the early stages of interpretation and application. Many lawyers who are not specialists in this field may also find it useful.

The book deals with legislation directly concerned with the various problems generally accepted as coming under the rather loosely defined heading of 'pollution'—disposal of waste, water pollution, noise, air pollution and so on—as in force on 1 January 1979. Related matters such as public health generally, land drainage and water supply, which are complex subjects in their own right, are not dealt with; nor is the Health and Safety at Work Act 1974, except where it deals with the control of atmospheric pollution. 'Industrial health and safety' aspects of air pollution, noise and waste disposal are left to books specialising in this area. However, the exclusion of these topics is not to be taken as an intention to minimise their importance or indicate that there are no controls over them.

Town and country planning legislation and the legal controls over radioactive materials are only briefly discussed: the former subject is too broad to allow more than certain directly relevant matters to be dealt with, while in the latter the law is of a highly technical nature. Similarly, the construction and use of motor vehicles is dealt with only briefly.

Given the complexity of the legislation, the book itself is inevitably detailed and complex; nevertheless, it is believed that it will meet a need as a straightforward exposition of 'what the law is' with regard to the control of industrial pollution.

University of Aston in Birmingham   Andrew Walker
January, 1979

Table of Statutes

Table of Statutory Instruments

Table of Cases

Control of Pollution Act 1974

Commencement in England and Wales

The following provisions of the Control of Pollution Act 1974 had not been brought into force on 1 January 1979:

Part I	s1
	s15

Part II	ss31-42
	ss45-48
	ss51-55

The following provisions of the Act had only partially been brought into force on 1 January 1979:

Part I	s12
	s13
	s14
	s18
	s24
	s27
	s28

INTRODUCTION

Concern over pollution and the problems of environmental protection is not new, but over the last few years much greater attention has been focussed on them. One result of this has been that the law relating to pollution and allied problems has been amended and extended.

The law on pollution control is one of the means used to attain an acceptable standard of environmental protection. In very general terms the law lays down rules which define what is an acceptable standard of behaviour. Failure to comply with the rules can have legal consequences which fall into two categories. If this failure causes injury or damage to someone, then, in certain circumstances, the wrongdoer will be civilly liable, ie, he must compensate the person who has been injured or suffered the damage. Alternatively, or frequently additionally, failure to comply with the law might involve a breach of criminal law with consequent criminal liability and the possibility of prosecution in the criminal courts. An act which causes pollution might well come in both categories.

This book concentrates on that part of the law which, if broken, might involve criminal liability. It is felt that this is likely to be of much more practical relevance in view of the increase in the detailed and complex legislation.

As a matter of principle, if there is a failure to comply with the requirements of the law, then the law can be regarded as having failed in one of its main objectives which is to ensure that people behave in a certain manner. This positive aspect of the law is much more important than the rather negative one which makes provision for punishment should a contravention occur. However, at an operational level, the necessity for compliance is not regarded in such an abstract fashion, but much more practically. If the law is not complied with, unpleasant consequences in the form of criminal proceedings and punishment may follow.

As a general rule, English law imposes liability on a person who fails to comply with the law, and when the liability of individuals is in issue few problems arise. However, as a result of the structure

1

of modern industry, the person carrying on an activity and who, in the eyes of the law, is the person responsible will often be a company rather than an individual. A company itself cannot act, but only acts through its directors, managers and other employees and so, if it incurs criminal liability, it will be because one of them has done something or failed to do something.

It is obviously one of the functions of management to ensure that the affairs of the company for which they are responsible are conducted in such a manner that no breach of the law is caused, particularly since, in some circumstances, this can result not only in punishment in the form of a fine but also in the revocation of a licence or in a court order to discontinue an activity. In many cases, however, the legislation also contains provisions which make the manager or employee who by his act or default renders the company liable, also guilty of an offence and liable to be proceeded against and punished.

To avoid these consequences, people in positions of responsibility within an organisation should ensure that its activities are conducted in accordance with the law. In order that this may be done, a knowledge of the law is necessary, but there is no easy answer to the question of what must be done to ensure that the requirements of the law are complied with. This is because of the approach adopted in this country to environmental protection legislation.

The legislation on pollution control, including the Control of Pollution Act 1974, does not contain a definition of pollution; for present purposes it is proposed to define it as occurring when man's activities have as their result, either directly or indirectly, an adverse effect on the environment which is unacceptable.

Thus it can be seen that pollution is a consequence of an activity rather than something which arises independently, and that the way in which the law attempts to control it is by controlling activities which are potentially polluting.

The direct controls can be divided into two broad categories:

(a) Where the result of an activity is pollution, the law requires steps to be taken to ensure that the pollution ceases.

(b) Where an activity is proposed, the law requires it to be carried out in such a way that no pollution will be caused. If it is impossible to carry out the activity and cause no pollution, the activity will be prohibited.

Examples of the first approach can be seen in the legislation on statutory nuisances and noise reduction notices. Examples of the second can be seen in the use of consents for discharges to inland waters and in the necessity for disposal licences in the case of the disposal of waste on land.

To ensure that an activity does not cause pollution, and thus stays within the law, it must not have an unacceptable adverse effect on the environment, but it is not possible to define precisely at what point the effect on the environment becomes unacceptable. Generally, English law in this matter does not lay down standards in precise terms but rather tends to adopt vague formulae such as that 'the best practicable means' must be used to prevent pollution. Alternatively, an activity which might be polluting will be prohibited unless the consent of a licensing authority has been obtained, and an authority has a power to attach to its consent conditions designed to prevent pollution.

A knowledge of the law can provide answers to certain questions such as 'Are there any legal controls over what it is proposed to do?' If the answer is in the affirmative, it can then provide general information as to what must be done to comply with the law. What the law does not do is to state in precise terms what must then be done. For example, it does not define what are 'the best practicable means' in a particular case, or what conditions should be attached to a consent. It is left to the appropriate licensing or enforcing authority to decide on the details in each case. This approach allows the relevant authority to respond in the light of the particular circumstances of a specific case, and also allows, for example, for the imposition of gradually changing standards when new technology provides more effective means for preventing pollution.

Although the law does not define what must be done, information on current practice is available in various Government publications such as the Pollution Papers and the Waste Management Papers. Pollution Paper No 11, *Environmental Standards: A Description of United Kingdom Practice* (HMSO 1977), states that:

> ... the United Kingdom adopts a pragmatic approach to environmental control and standard setting. It is not general practice for statutes to specify standards either for particular emissions or for general environmental quality. Authorities which in practice often work to fairly uniform standards or within widely accepted limits are normally given discretion to set their own local standards. The approach adopted is that these standards should be practicable having regard among other things to local conditions and circumstances, to the current state of scientific and technical knowledge, and to the financial implications ...

3

Thus, in general terms, the law states that no pollution will be caused and no criminal offence committed, provided that an activity is carried on in such a way that its impact on the environment is limited to an acceptable level. Various bodies are given discretion to fix this level by reference to various factors. So that they may be better informed on matters relevant to deciding these standards, authorities now have wide powers to compel the furnishing of information, and these are enforceable by criminal sanctions.

In conclusion, two points need to be stressed: firstly, that a knowledge of the law is necessary; secondly, that this knowledge cannot provide easy answers to what should be done because of the flexible nature of the controls over pollution. The details of what must be done must be ascertained by reference to non-legal matters such as the current practice of pollution control, financial considerations and local conditions, but these must be examined within the framework of the law. Thus, although a knowledge of the law cannot provide precise answers as to what must be done, until the law is known it is not possible to establish exactly how its requirements may be complied with.

CHAPTER ONE

COMMON LAW AND STATUTORY NUISANCES

Common Law

The English law of pollution control is derived from two separate sources. These are common law, the body of principles developed by judges in cases, and statute law, the body of rules laid down by or with the authority of Parliament in Acts and Statutory Instruments. The latter is more important from a practical point of view, and is much more complex. However, common law will be examined first since it provides the background against which the legislation developed, and it still lays down obligations which, if broken, may lead to a substantial claim for damages by an injured party.

The part of common law most relevant to pollution control is the law of tort, which can be broadly defined as that branch of the law which deals with civil wrongs which are not solely a breach of contract. In certain circumstances the law gives a person who has been injured by the actions of another a right to be compensated for the loss which he has sustained. There is, however, no general principle whereby a person whose actions cause damage to another must compensate that other person.

The injured person's right to compensation is limited in two respects. Firstly, to establish that the wrongdoer is liable, there must have been a breach of a legal duty owed by him or, conversely, the injured party's legal rights must have been infringed. Secondly, where this first element is established, the law limits the damages for which the injured party may claim, and excludes damages which are too remote. Thus there are two broad questions: Can an injured party claim damages, and if so, how much? Will a person who wishes to carry on an activity lay himself open to a claim for damages and, more importantly, how can he carry on that activity without incurring any potential liability?

Trespass to Land

This is the simplest tort, and also the tort which will be least likely to cause liability today. Trespass to land consists of the placing of any object on the land of another person without his consent, even though no damage is caused. In legal theory it is the placing of the object on the land which gives the plaintiff a right to claim damages, since that action, with nothing more, constitutes an infringement of the owner's rights. Although if no damage had been caused the plaintiff would win the case, the amount of damages awarded would only be a token sum in recognition of the fact that his legal rights had been infringed.

The practical limit on the application of this tort is that the damage caused must be direct and not consequential. Of direct injuries it can be said that the defendant committed the act complained of, and of consequential damages, that the injury occurred as a result of his action. For example, deliberately to place rubbish on someone else's property would be trespass. To pile rubbish on one's own property which, as the result of wind and weather, collapses and overflows onto the land of another is not trespass, whatever else it may be. In other words, trespass covers the case where the defendant commits a wrongful act, although in most cases brought today the defendant has committed an act which has had harmful consequences.

An example of the difficulties of applying trespass to modern situations can be seen in the case of Esso Petroleum v Southport Corporation. When the defendant's oil tanker ran aground, the master, in order to save the ship, jettisoned some of the cargo and this was carried by wind and tide onto the plaintiff's beach. Throughout the proceedings there was doubt as to whether the damage was direct or consequential, but the better view was that it was consequential since the master's actions merely brought about a situation in which oil might or might not have been carried onto the beach. Therefore, regardless of other remedies which might have been possible (and because of various factors in this case, including procedural ones, none were), it was impossible to establish liability in trespass. However, legal proceedings might now be possible in a case of this kind under the legislation concerning oil pollution at sea.

Negligence

The tort of negligence, as the name implies, is concerned with the situation where careless conduct causes harm. Mere carelessness on the part of the defendant is not sufficient to render him liable since negligence has a definite legal meaning, although there will be many cases where the legal concept and the commonsense concept of negligence are identical.

To establish the plaintiff's entitlement to a remedy, it must be shown that:

(a) The defendant owes the plaintiff a duty of care. Whether or not a duty exists is a complicated question, but for present purposes the position can be summarised: if it is reasonably foreseeable that your acts or omissions will result in harm to some person unless you take reasonable care, then you are under a duty to take reasonable care to ensure that this harm does not occur.

(b) In the circumstances, the defendant failed to take reasonable care. Whether he did or not is something which has to be decided upon an examination of all the relevant information. The courts have evolved various criteria which may be applied to ascertain whether or not reasonable care has been taken. One approach has been to say that reasonable care is taken if foreseeable harm is guarded against, but whether harm is foreseeable or not is frequently very difficult to decide. An alternative is to use the concept of risk. This involves the weighing of the gravity and likelihood of any potential injury against the precautions required to eliminate that risk. In other words, the greater the risk, the greater are the precautions necessary to establish that reasonable care has been taken. Whether or not reasonable care has been taken is assessed in the context of current society. For example, technological advance may have the result that it becomes necessary to take increased precautions in order to establish that reasonable care has been taken.

(c) The damage suffered by the plaintiff was caused by the defendant's failure to take reasonable care.

As in most areas of law, the onus of proof falls on the plaintiff who must establish the existence of a duty of care, and that it was a failure to take reasonable care which caused the damage. It is not up to the defendant to prove that he was not negligent. However, this rule may cause difficulty and hardship if the circumstances surrounding the accident are solely within the knowledge of the defendant, when the plaintiff can show that an accident happened, but can prove nothing more. It may then be possible to invoke the doctrine of *res ipsa loquitur* (the thing speaks for itself) to assist the plaintiff, so that if the accident is proved, it is up to the defendant to show that he was not negligent. If he cannot do so, then the plaintiff will win his case. For the burden of proof to be thus shifted, the following conditions must be fulfilled:

(1) The circumstances which caused the accident must have been under the control of the defendant.
(2) The accident must have been such that it would not have happened in the ordinary course of events had those in control exercised proper care.

Thus, the event itself will be sufficient proof of negligence unless the contrary is proved. It should be noted that the defendant does not have to prove how the accident happened; he only has to establish that he himself was not negligent.

Nuisance

Most cases of pollution will come under the tort of nuisance. There are two sorts of nuisance, public nuisance and private nuisance; although it is the law of private nuisance that is particularly relevant, mention must first be made of public nuisance.

Public nuisance

The essence of a public nuisance is that it is a criminal offence consisting of an act or omission which materially affects the comfort or the convenience of the public. Where such an offence is committed, it would be unreasonable to expect one person to incur the trouble and expense of taking action to restrain the nuisance, so the community does so. The principal remedy is for the Attorney General to take proceedings, although by statute a local authority may initiate them. An individual may sue for damages only if he has suffered loss over and above that suffered by the community, at large, as, for example, where the activity has caused annoyance to people generally, but where the individual has been physically injured.

An example of this is the case of Halsey v Esso Petroleum Co. Ltd, in which smuts from the defendant's oil refinery damaged clothes belonging to the plantiff which were hanging in his garden, and his car which was standing in the road outside his house. The plaintiff was able to obtain damages in private nuisance in respect of his clothes, and in public nuisance in respect of his car.

Private nuisance

Private nuisance is an area of law which has developed to regulate the conflicting interests of individuals; the one element it has in common with public nuisance is inconvenience or annoyance.

An exact definition of private nuisance is difficult, but the essential factor is that there must be interference with the use or enjoyment of property. The question which has to be resolved is this: if the defendant is carrying on some activity which adversely affects his neighbour's property or its use, can the affected party restrain the activity and/or claim damages for the injury or inconvenience suffered?

Many of the cases which have developed the tort of nuisance deal with what is now called pollution—noise, as in Allison v Merton, Sutton and Wandsworth AHA (see p 89), smells, smoke and fumes as in St Helen's Smelting Co. v Tipping (see below), and the pollution of watercourses.

It is possible to identify two sorts of injury which give rise to an action for nuisance, to which somewhat different principles apply. The first is where the defendant's activities interfere with the use or enjoyment of property. The second is where the activities cause some physical damage to the property.

It must be stressed that since nuisance is an interference with property rights, only a person with some interest in the property affected may take action to obtain a remedy.

Interference with use or enjoyment of property

In certain circumstances if a person's activities interfere with the use or enjoyment of the property of another, then those activities may be restrained and compensation awarded. However, not every interference will provide grounds for action.

For an interference to be actionable, there must be substantial interference. Mere annoyance will not suffice. The standard to be applied is an objective one: would a reasonable man object in these circumstances? The nature of the locality is relevant in that a person must be expected to suffer the level of inconvenience which is reasonable in that locality. For instance, a person living in a city centre cannot expect the same quiet and seclusion as if he were living in a small country village. In the case of Sturges v Bridgman where the plaintiff, a physician, obtained a remedy in respect of

9

noise caused by heavy machinery which adversely affected the use of his consulting room, Thesiger LJ said, 'What would be a nuisance in Belgrave Square would not necessarily be a nuisance in Bermondsey.'

It is important to note the use of the word 'necessarily' since certain things would be a nuisance in Bermondsey if they were over and above the normal level of inconvenience suffered there. Thus, although the nature of the locality is relevant, it does not mean, for example, that industry can do what it likes in an industrial area.

Damage to property

Different considerations apply in respect of this branch of the tort. While a person living in an industrial area can be said to assume the normal inconveniences involved in living in such an area, there is no rule which allows a person to use his property so as to inflict damage on the property of another.

Unlike interference with the use and enjoyment of property, the nature of the locality is irrelevant. For example, in St Helen's Smelting Co. v Tipping, mentioned above, the plaintiff owned a large estate near the defendant's property where copper smelting was carried on. The fumes from the smelter caused damage to the plaintiff's trees and shrubs. He won his action, the court holding that the industrial nature of the area was irrelevant since what was alleged was physical damage to property.

Although certain defences are available to a defendant in proceedings for nuisance, it must be noted that certain matters are not defences. In particular, it is not a defence to show that the activities complained of were for the public benefit, nor that where they were carried on was a convenient place. Nor is it a defence to show that reasonable care has been taken.

Therefore, this tort is wider than negligence but, unlike nuisance, there is no restriction in negligence that only persons with some proprietary interest may sue.

Two defences of particular relevance can be considered. The first is prescription. Where a nuisance has been in existence for at least twenty years, the defendant acquires an unimpeachable right to carry on those activities which caused the nuisance. They must have been carried out openly and with the knowledge of the person affected. Furthermore, it is not sufficient that the activities have continued for twenty years. The nuisance itself must have existed for twenty years.

10

There are today two important limitations to the principle of prescription. Firstly, it is not possible to obtain a prescriptive right to commit a public nuisance. Secondly, it is not possible to obtain a prescriptive right to commit an act which contravenes a statutory prohibition. Since virtually every act which might be called polluting is also a criminal act, it is almost impossible to obtain a prescriptive right to pollute.

A second defence is that of statutory authorisation. In many cases a statute authorises an activity which would otherwise be unlawful and this relieves the body carrying it on, usually a public authority, from liability in nuisance. Such provisions are interpreted to mean that the body carrying on the activity will be under no liability to persons affected unless it can be shown that there was negligence.

For example, the Public Health Act 1936 s31 states that a local authority shall so discharge its functions under this Part of the Act (relating to the provision of public sewers) as not to create a nuisance. In Smeaton v Ilford Corporation, a case concerning the overflow of sewage from a public sewer, Upjohn J said, 'So far as this court is concerned, it must be taken as settled that the proper construction to be given to this section is to exclude liability for escapes in the absence of negligence'.

The Rule in Rylands v Fletcher

An occupier of land who brings onto it and keeps there anything likely to do damage if it escapes, is bound to prevent its escape and is liable for the direct consequences of any escape, even if he has not been negligent. This is an example of strict liability in that liability does not depend on fault, and injuries arising out of the dangerous situation are alone sufficient to make the defendant liable.

For the rule to apply, various conditions must be fulfilled. Firstly, there must be the storage of a dangerous thing on the land, ie, a substance likely to cause damage if it escapes. Certain things, such as noxious chemicals, will always be dangerous for this purpose. Others, such as water, may or may not be dangerous, depending on the circumstances. It has also been stated that there must be a non-natural use of the land. The definition of this has caused problems, but it can be summarised as being an extraordinary or abnormal use which involves an increased risk to others. The final point to note is that the rule only applies to substances or things brought onto the land and has no application to things naturally on the land, however dangerous they might be. Secondly, there must be an

11

escape beyond the boundaries of the defendant's land. If the injury occurs on his land, then the rule does not apply. Finally, the escape must cause damage.

Provided these requirements are satisfied, the defendant will be liable for all the direct consequences of the escape, although he might have taken all reasonable care to guard against an accident.

However, several defences or exceptions to the rule have been developed. In particular, it is a defence to show that the escape was caused by the act of a third party, unless that act was foreseeable, in which case any liability will be in negligence. An Act of God is also a defence, but in practice it will rarely succeed. An Act of God is a natural occurrence so unlikely that no one could possibly have foreseen or guarded against it. In England an earthquake would probably be an Act of God, whereas a torrential rainstorm causing flooding would not. The defence of statutory authorisation already mentioned in connection with nuisance also applies to the Rule in Rylands v Fletcher.

Breach of Statutory Duty

Breach of statutory duty is an area of tort which has elements of both common law and statute law. Problems can arise where a statute imposes a duty, usually enforceable by criminal sanctions. If a person fails to carry out that duty and causes damage to another, can that other party claim compensation?

Nowadays there is a tendency for statutes to make plain the extent to which a breach of such a duty gives the right to compensation, as in the Health and Safety at Work Act 1974 (see p 126), and the Control of Pollution Act 1974 (see p 86). Both have specific provisions covering this, but in many cases statutes are silent on compensation. To resolve the problems the courts have evolved several general principles.

If a statute is passed for the benefit of the public at large as opposed to a class or section of society, then there is a presumption that no private rights are conferred. If a specific remedy is given in the Act, as, for example, a right of appeal to an administrative agency, it is presumed that that is the only available remedy. Furthermore, if the provisions of the Act are enforceable by criminal sanctions, then there is a presumption, although not conclusive, that no private rights are conferred. Finally, the courts will look at the purpose of the statute. If the purpose is to protect a particular class, and a member of that class suffers damage as a result of a proscribed activity or breach of duty, then it is likely that the courts will hold that a private right of action exists. Perhaps the best example of this is the Factories Acts, where the courts have held that breaches of duties enforced by criminal sanctions give an injured employee a right to obtain damages.

Vicarious Liability

If an employee commits a tort during the course of his employment, the injured person may sue both the employer and the employee. For the employer to be liable, the employee must actually be an employee and not an independent contractor, and he must have been acting in the course of his employment. If he is acting for his own purposes and these are totally unconnected with his employer's business, then the employer will probably not be liable.

Remedies

Damages

The principal remedy for an injured person in tort is the award of damages for loss caused by the defendant's wrongful act. Broadly, the award must compensate the plaintiff for injury caused by the defendant's act which was reasonably foreseeable. The exact injury need not be foreseeable, nor its extent. It is sufficient if the general nature of the injury is foreseeable. It should be noted, however, that in assessing damage for injury caused under the Rule in Rylands v Fletcher, foreseeability is not the test, but directness is. Did the defendant's actions cause the damage? In most cases the tests of foreseeability and directness will provide the same answer. Any damage falling outside these definitions is too remote to allow the plaintiff to claim compensation.

The sum to which the plaintiff is entitled may be reduced by the principle of contributory negligence contained in the Law Reform (Contributory Negligence) Act 1945. The broad principle is as follows: if someone suffers harm partly as the result of his own fault and partly as the result of another's, the damages to which he is entitled are reduced by the amount that the court feels reflects the claimant's share in the responsibility for the damage. Thus the court can apportion both blame and damages.

Injunction

An injunction is a court order restraining the defendant from doing something or, more rarely, compelling him to do something. It will only be granted if the court feels that an award of damages would not adequately compensate the plaintiff. An example of this would be where the defendant shows no intention of discontinuing the activities complained of.

An injunction is most likely to be used in cases of nuisance since these are usually continuing states of affairs rather than isolated acts. Damages can be awarded for previous injuries, particularly in nuisance cases, and also an injunction can be granted to prevent a recurrence.

Since, except in trespass, injury is an essential ingredient of torts, the plaintiff will not establish his right to damages until the injury has been suffered. Only in exceptional circumstances will an injunction be awarded to stop an injury which has not yet happened. Such an injunction (*quia timet*) will only be granted if there is a large degree of probability that the injury will be inflicted, will be substantial, will shortly occur, and damages will not be adequate compensation for such injury.

Abatement

This remedy is of particular relevance in relation to nuisance. In many circumstances a person who is a victim of a nuisance may himself take steps to abate it. However, such a course of action is inadvisable unless there are exceptional circumstances since it may lead to a breach of the peace. Moreover, if eventually it transpired that the matter abated did not amount in law to a nuisance, then the person who abated it would be liable to compensate the other party for damage done.

Statutory Nuisances

The Public Health Act 1936 contains a quicker and simpler procedure than the common law of tort to restrain certain activities which are hazardous to health, known as statutory nuisances.

The responsibility for dealing with these is laid on local authorities, although in certain circumstances an individual may take action. For these purposes a local authority is a district council, a London borough council, the Common Council of the City of London, the Sub-Treasurer of the Inner Temple, and the Under Treasurer of the Middle Temple.

Definition

Matters subject to the statutory nuisance procedure considered relevant in connection with pollution control are:

(a) Premises in such a state that they are prejudicial to health or are a nuisance. Presumably this would be similar to the common law test of nuisance, that is, substantial interference with the enjoyment of property, or damage to property.
(b) Accumulations or deposits which are prejudicial to health or are a nuisance.
(c) Dust or effluvia caused by a trade, business, manufacture or process which are prejudicial to health or are a nuisance to the inhabitants of the neighbourhood.
(d) Any other matters declared to be a statutory nuisance. These include:

Under s259: (i) Any pond, pool, ditch or watercourse which is so foul or in such a condition as to be prejudicial to health or to constitute a nuisance; (ii) Any watercourse not ordinarily navigated by goods vessels which is so choked or silted as to obstruct the flow of water and thereby cause a nuisance or give rise to a condition prejudicial to health.

Under s101: Certain smoke nuisances. These provisions were replaced by the Clean Air Act 1956 which introduced a new system of control over emissions from chimneys but retained certain emissions as statutory nuisances subject to the controls of the 1936 Act (see p 140).

Under the Noise Abatement Act 1960: Noise was made a statutory nuisance subject to the 1936 Act controls. The Noise Abatement Act has been replaced by similar provisions in the Control of Pollution Act 1974, and noise is no longer a statutory nuisance under the 1936 Act (see p 89).

There is a restriction on action by the local authority, in that if it is proposed to take action under (b) or (c), and it would be possible for action to be taken under the Alkali Act (see p 111), the local authority must first obtain the consent of the Secretary of State. **s92**

Abatement Notices

Where a local authority is satisfied that a statutory nuisance exists, it must serve an abatement notice on the person by whose act, default or sufferance the nuisance arises or continues. If he cannot be found it must be served on the owner or occupier of the premises on which the nuisance arises. It must require the person on whom it is served to abate the nuisance and to take such steps and execute such works as may be necessary for that purpose. Where the nuisance is caused by a structural fault in a building, the notice must be served on the owner.

If the person who caused the nuisance cannot be found and it is clear that the nuisance does not arise or continue as the result of the act, default or sufferance of the owner or occupier, the local authority itself may take steps to abate it and prevent a recurrence. **s93**

Nuisance Orders

If an abatement notice is not complied with, or the local authority thinks that the nuisance, although abated, is likely to recur, the authority must take proceedings in a magistrate's court for a nuisance order. If the court is satisfied that the abatement notice has not been complied with or that a recurrence is likely, it must make a nuisance order for one or both of the following purposes:

(a) For the defendant to comply with the abatement notice or otherwise abate the nuisance within a specified time, and to carry out any necessary works.

(b) To prohibit the recurrence of the nuisance and to require any works to be executed which are necessary for that purpose.

The court may include such terms in a nuisance order as it thinks fit, provided that they are clear, precise, and capable of being implemented. In addition to the making of the nuisance order, the court may impose a maximum fine of £200 on the defendant. Furthermore, where the nuisance was in existence at the time the abatement notice was served, and continued or was likely to recur at the time proceedings for a nuisance order were begun, then, whether or not it was continuing or was likely to recur at the date of the hearing, the court must order the defendant to pay the authority the cost of the proceedings to obtain the nuisance order.

There are two defences available to a defendant in proceedings for a nuisance order. Where the proceedings are in respect of deposits or accumulations which are a nuisance, it is a defence to show that they were necessary for the effectual carrying on of a business or manufacture, were not kept longer than was necessary, and that the best practicable means were used to prevent them from being prejudicial to health or a nuisance. When there are

16

proceedings in respect of dust or effluvia, it will be a defence to show that the best practicable means were used to prevent or counteract their effect.

The maximum penalties for a contravention of a nuisance order are a fine of £400, and a fine of £50 per day on which the nuisance continues after a conviction in respect of it. **ss94, 95**

Default Powers of Local Authorities

Where there are proceedings for a nuisance order after non-compliance with an abatement notice, and the person by whose act or default the nuisance arose or the owner or occupier of the premises cannot be found, the court can address the nuisance order to the local authority who may then execute it. In addition, where a nuisance order has been made but has not been complied with, the local authority may abate the nuisance and do whatever is necessary to execute the order.

Where a local authority carries out the operations under any of these powers, it can recover any expenses incurred from the person to whom the nuisance order was addressed, if it was addressed to a person other than the local authority. Where the order was addressed to the local authority, any expenses can be recovered from the person by whose act or default the nuisance was caused. **ss 94–96**

Action by Individuals

A person aggrieved by a statutory nuisance may himself initiate legal proceedings against the person creating the nuisance. Thereafter, the procedure is the same as in the case of local authority proceedings for a nuisance order. After hearing the local authority, the court is empowered to order it to abate the nuisance, and the local authority can then recover the costs of so doing.

In two recent cases the right of an individual to take proceedings was considered by the Divisional Court in R v Newham Justices ex p Hunt and R v Oxted Justices ex p Franklin. It was held in these two cases that an individual may proceed either by way of information or complaint, and that there is no need for an abatement notice to have been served in respect of the alleged nuisance, ie, when an individual wishes to take action he can apply immediately to the court for a nuisance order, whereas a local authority first has to serve an abatement notice. **s99**

Miscellaneous Provisions

If a statutory nuisance is caused by the acts or defaults of two or more persons, proceedings can be taken against any or all of them. A person can be ordered to discontinue an activity which contributes to the nuisance, even though his actions alone would not constitute a nuisance. Where only some of the persons responsible are proceeded against, they can recover a proportion of the cost from the others, and the court has the power to make such apportionment as seems fair and reasonable. **s97**

If a nuisance in an authority's area arises from a cause situated outside its area, it may take proceedings to restrain it, but these must be held in a court having jurisdiction in the place where the nuisance arises. **s98**

If the authority is of the opinion that summary proceedings provide an inadequate remedy, it may take proceedings in the High Court even though it has not itself suffered any damage. **s100**

The Public Health (Recurring Nuisances) Act 1969

The law on statutory nuisances was slightly extended in 1969 by this Act. Where a local authority is satisfied that a statutory nuisance has occurred and is likely to recur, it may serve a prohibition notice. Unlike an abatement notice under the 1936 Act, a prohibition notice can be served if the nuisance has existed, and is likely to recur, although at the time of service of the notice it does not exist. This notice must be served on the owner of the premises if the nuisance is caused by the structure of the premises, and in any other case on the person whose act, default or sufferance caused the nuisance or, if he cannot be found, on the owner or occupier of the premises.

A prohibition notice prohibits the recurrence of the nuisance, and can require the person on whom it is served to take such steps as may be necessary to prevent a recurrence. This notice may also specify works to prevent the recurrence.

A prohibition notice may be served whether or not an abatement notice has been served, although an abatement notice and a prohibition notice may be contained in the same document. **s1**

Where the nuisance recurs after the service of the prohibition notice, or the notice is not complied with in some other respect, the authority may take proceedings in the magistrate's court for a nuisance order, when the provisions of the 1936 Act relating to nuisance orders apply, with two modifications:

Under the 1969 Act only a local authority has a right to take action. An individual is given no rights. As far as costs are concerned, the court can award them to the local authority if at the date of the commencement of the proceedings the nuisance had recurred, or the prohibition notice had not been complied with, and in either case the nuisance was likely to recur, whether or not at the date of the hearing the nuisance was likely to recur or the failure to comply continued. **ss2, 3**

Enforcement

For the powers available to a local authority to enforce the statutory nuisance provisions (see p 151).

Conclusion

The common law principles outlined at the beginning of the chapter were developed over a long period. However, by the first half of the 19th century it was becoming increasingly apparent that the common law was inadequate to deal with the problems thrown up by the Industrial Revolution.

For various reasons common law is defective in combating pollution. It is especially concerned with the protection of property rights, particularly in connection with nuisance. What is more, common law tends to be individualistic, protecting the rights of an individual as an individual, and leaving it to him to decide whether or not to take legal proceedings.

The basic principle of common law is compensation rather than regulation, as can be seen in the fact that in most torts actual injury is a necessary prerequisite to the right to obtain compensation. To say that common law has no regulatory function would be an overstatement, since the prospect of heavy damages against someone will undoubtedly influence his conduct, nor will he want an injunction granted against him.

Therefore, as stated, common law is basically concerned with compensation and the protection of private rights. If an individual whose rights are affected is unable or unwilling to take action, then no other person can do so. For example, if a river is polluted, only the riparian landowners or persons who have some other right such as a fishery can take action. A local amenity society, for instance, would have no right to take action.

As common law's inadequacies were exposed, Parliament began to intervene, tentatively at first, but with more stringent measures later, providing additional controls and remedies. However common law is the foundation on which the mass of legislation controlling pollution is based and it remains the principal remedy today whereby anyone who is injured by the acts of another may claim compensation.

CHAPTER TWO

THE POLLUTION OF
INLAND WATERS AND THE
DISPOSAL OF LIQUID WASTE

A.   POLLUTION OF INLAND WATERS

The common law on the protection of rights in rivers and watercourses is fairly well developed. Broadly speaking, a riparian owner,
that is the owner of land forming a bank of a river, has a right to
receive unpolluted water in its natural state in the river flowing
into his property. If a person upstream pollutes the river, the
landowner downstream may sue in trespass or in nuisance, or
possibly in negligence or under the Rule in Rylands v Fletcher for
damages in respect of past pollution, and to obtain an injunction
to restrain further pollution (see p 5). However, as mentioned in
Chapter 1, only the riparian owner or the owner of other property
rights can sue in respect of damage done to those rights. It should
be noted that this is limited to water flowing in defined channels.
There is no similar right in respect of water percolating in undefined
underground channels.

Statutory intervention began in the early 19th century when the
public health movement began to exert its influence in the improvement of water supplies, and tackled the problem of sewage and its
disposal. The first major piece of legislation dealing with water
pollution was the Rivers Pollution Prevention Act 1876. However,
for many years water pollution was only considered as one aspect
of the wider problems of public health, and it was not until after
the Second World War that its importance in its own right was
recognised. Two distinct strands can be seen, in the development
of an administrative machine and the development of the legislation
which various bodies had to enforce.

Briefly, the history of the authorities is as follows. In 1948 a system of River Boards was set up. These were replaced by River Authorities in 1963, and a central body, the Water Resources Board, was formed. In 1973 there was a further change when the Water Act replaced the River Authorities with nine English Regional Water Authorities and the Welsh Water Development Authority. These assumed all the functions of the River Authorities, together with the responsibilities of other bodies, and the new National Water Council replaced the Water Resources Board.

At the time of writing a White Paper, *The Water Industry in England and Wales: the Next Steps* (Cmnd 6876) is under consideration, which, if implemented, will effect further alterations to the system, in particular the introduction of the National Water Authority, a new central body which will assume responsibility for the central strategic planning of water resources.

The legislation these bodies have had to administer has developed over the same period of time. In 1951 the Rivers (Prevention of Pollution) Act replaced the 1876 Act, and controls were extended by the Rivers (Prevention of Pollution) Act 1961. The Clean Rivers (Estuaries and Tidal Waters) Act 1960 extended similar controls to specified coastal waters. Both the Water Resources Act 1963 and the Water Act 1973 were concerned with problems of water, and other pieces of legislation dealt with specific problems such as land drainage and fisheries, and incidentally with water pollution. (For instance, the Salmon and Freshwater Fisheries Act 1923 was replaced by the Salmon and Freshwater Fisheries Act 1975 which contains a provision stating that it is an offence to cause or knowingly permit to flow, or put or cause or knowingly permit to be put into any waters containing fish, or into any tributaries of waters containing fish, any liquid or solid matter to such an extent as to cause the waters to be poisonous or injurious to fish or the spawning grounds, spawn or food of fish. **s4**)

Most of the existing legislation will be replaced by the relevant provisions of the Control of Pollution Act 1974, but as yet none of those dealing with water pollution have been brought into effect.

Existing Legislation

The Rivers (Prevention of Pollution) Acts 1951 and 1961

These Acts can be considered as dealing with two separate matters, (i) criminal offences for polluting rivers, in the main an updating of previous provisions, and (ii) an innovation, the licensing of outlets and discharges to streams. Both of these Acts will be dealt with together, but the broad division is that the 1961 Act extended the controls of the 1951 Act concerning licensing to those discharges and outlets which were exempt from control under the 1951 Act.

Polluting matter

(i) It is an offence to cause or knowingly permit to enter a stream any poisonous, noxious or polluting matter, or to cause or knowingly permit to enter a stream any matter so as to tend either directly or in combination with similar acts to impede the proper flow of the water in a manner leading to or likely to lead to a substantial aggravation of pollution due to other causes, or of the consequences of such pollution.

However, there are certain exceptions. There is no offence if water raised or drained from a mine is discharged into a stream in the same condition in which it was raised or drained, but the Secretary of State has a power to remove this exemption in relation to specified streams. Also, no offence is committed if the solid waste from a mine or quarry falls into a stream, provided that the original deposit was made with the consent of the authority (which must not be unreasonably withheld), that no other site is reasonably practicable and that all reasonable steps are taken to ensure that the waste does not fall into the stream. **s2/51**

There have been two recent cases on this section. They are important because they will have relevance under the new legislation and illustrate the difference between the two separate sets of offences, causing pollution and knowingly to permit it.

In Alphacell Ltd v Woodward the question was whether a person could be guilty even though he had taken all reasonable precautions, and unknown to him the river was polluted. In this case the appellants, Alphacell Ltd, were involved in papermaking, and this involved the washing of fibres. The water, after washing, was piped to two settling tanks and recycled. To prevent an overflow to the nearby river there were two pumps in the tanks. One switched on automatically when a certain level was reached. The other, a standby pump, could be switched on manually. In the event of an overflow a channel led directly to the river. The pumps were inspected every weekend by a fitter, and each pump was protected by a filter to prevent it from becoming clogged. On one occasion there was an overflow, and the river was polluted. The pumps were found to be clogged with vegetation although they had been inspected the previous weekend, and there had been a regular

23

inspection on the day of the incident. Nothing similar had ever occurred before. The appellant's conviction for causing the pollution was upheld.

The building and operation of the settling tanks with an overflow channel directly to the river and the use of the pumps with no emergency safeguard had led directly to the overflow and subsequent pollution. There was no evidence of an Act of God or of interference by a third party. Once the causal link had been established, there was no necessity for the prosecution to prove knowledge, intention or negligence.

This case can be contrasted with that of Price v Cromack. Price, the appellant, had entered into an agreement with a neighbouring landowner. This permitted effluent from the neighbour's property to accumulate on Price's property for dispersal, and two lagoons were built for this purpose. There was a crack in one of the lagoons, and this allowed the effluent to escape and be dissolved in the adjoining land, while a crack in the second lagoon permitted the effluent to pass into the first lagoon and in its turn to escape. The result was that the nearby river was badly polluted. On appeal Price's conviction for causing pollution was quashed. A statement made by Lord Wilberforce was cited by Lord Widgery: 'Causing involves some active operation or chain of operations involving as a result the pollution; knowingly permitting involves a failure to prevent, which failure must however be accompanied by knowledge.' The court's opinion was that had Price been charged with knowingly permitting the pollution, he would have had great difficulty in finding a defence.

(ii) It is an offence to clean the bed or channel of a stream of a deposit which has accumulated because of a dam, weir or sluice by causing the deposit to be carried away in suspension by the stream. It is also an offence by wilful default to allow any vegetation uprooted or cut in the stream, or so near the stream that it falls in, to remain. No offence is committed under either of these, however, if the consent of the authority has been given. This consent must not be unreasonably withheld. **s4/51**

These provisions may be extended by the Secretary of State by order to tidal waters. Before he can act, an authority must make an application and notice of the intention to extend the Act must be published in the London Gazette. **s6/51**

24

Preventive measures

Where an authority is of the opinion that an offence under Polluting Matter above is likely to occur because of the use of land for the disposal or storage of any matter, or a proposed use of a stream for the disposal of any matter, or the use for the carriage of cargoes of a defective vessel from which poisonous, noxious or polluting matter might enter the stream, it may apply to the court for an order restraining the proposed activity. The court may make an order prohibiting such use, or permitting it on conditions designed to ensure that no pollution will result. The court can also order the person against whom the order is made to remove any material which has caused harm, and if he defaults the authority may remove it. **s3/51**

Consents to discharges and outlets: trade and sewage effluent

It is an offence to use an outlet for the discharge of trade or sewage effluent to a stream or to make a discharge of such effluent to a stream without the consent of the water authority.

An application for a consent must specify the nature, composition, temperature and rate of discharge of the effluent. The authority can give its consent unconditionally or subject to conditions which cover the siting of an outlet and its construction and use, the nature, composition, temperature, volume and rate of discharge of the effluent, and the provision of manholes and inspection covers to facilitate the taking of samples.

The authority must keep consents under review, and make any necessary alterations in the conditions. A consent has to contain a statement to the effect that the conditions will not be varied within a specified period of not less than two years without the agreement of the person to whom it was given.

The authority must keep a register of the conditions attached to consents, and these must be open to inspection at all reasonable times by any person interested in the land or outlet, or any person authorised by him. This register is conclusive evidence of the conditions a person must observe in order not to commit an offence.

The use of a new outlet or the commencement of a new discharge without consent is an offence, as is a failure to observe any conditions attached to a consent. If a new outlet is brought into use or a new discharge is begun without it, then the authority may serve a notice on the offender imposing such conditions as might have been imposed had there been an application.

If an authority fails to give its reply to an application for consent within three months, consent is deemed to be given unconditionally. In the event of a dispute as to the reasonableness of conditions, or as to whether the authority is unreasonably withholding consent, an appeal may be made to the Secretary of State. **s7/51, ss1, 5–7/61**

Administrative provisions

The following provisions will remain in force after the Control of Pollution Act 1974 comes into effect.

Samples

A water authority may make an agreement with the occupier of land or premises from which effluent is discharged as to the point or points at which samples are to be taken of the effluent passing into the waters. If no agreement is made, the authority may apply to the Secretary of State who, after considering any representations made by the occupier of the land or anyone else interested, may fix the point at which samples are to be taken. From time to time the Secretary of State, on the application of the authority or the occupier of the land or premises, may review and vary any such decision. The authority must keep a register of such sampling points which must be open to inspection by any person the authority considers to be an interested party.

Until the contrary is proved, it will be presumed that a sample of effluent taken at a sampling point, or from a manhole or inspection chamber, or other place, is a sample of what was passing from the land or premises into the waters. **s10/61**

Disclosure of information

It is an offence to disclose information which has been furnished or obtained in connection with an application for consent or the imposition of conditions, including variations and references and applications to the Secretary of State, or which has been derived from a sample of effluent taken for the purpose of the Acts. Disclosure is authorised if:

(a) It is made with the consent of the person who gave the information.
(b) The information is derived from a sample, and disclosure is made with the consent of the person making the discharge.
(c) It is made for the purposes of the Acts or in connection with any proceedings, including references to the Secretary of State, or criminal proceedings, or the report of such proceedings.

However, none of this is to prevent the disclosure of information derived from a sample of water into which effluent is discharged. **s12/61**

The Clean Rivers (Estuaries and Tidal Waters) Act 1960

This Act extended the above controls over outlets and discharges to the tidal waters specified in the Schedule to the Act. The limits of the extensions are set out precisely, and it is not proposed to give details.

The Water Resources Act 1963

This Act gave authorities power to control discharges of effluent to underground strata. After 1 July 1965 it became an offence to discharge, without the authority's consent which must not be unreasonably withheld, any sewage or trade effluent or poisonous, noxious or polluting matter into any underground strata by means of a well, borehole or pipe. If, within three months or such longer period as may be agreed, the authority fails to consent to an application, it will be deemed to have been refused. An appeal against this decision may be made to the Secretary of State.

The consent may be given subject to conditions as to the nature, volume and composition of the effluent, the strata into which it may be discharged, measures for protecting other water in strata through which it might pass, and the provision of facilities for inspection. The authority may revoke a consent, or vary any conditions.

A register of consents must be kept, which must be open to public inspection, and is conclusive evidence of the terms of a consent. **ss72–74**

The Act also gave authorities additional powers. If any poisonous, noxious or polluting thing has entered a river as the result of an unforeseen circumstance or an accident. the authority can take whatever steps it thinks necessary to remove the matter and remedy the pollution. It has a right of entry to carry out its functions under the Act and, in the event of being denied access, may obtain entry by warrant from a magistrate.

Under s113 a water authority may take samples of effluent, and under s114 it can compel the furnishing of any information it may require from anyone who is abstracting water or discharging effluent. These two powers will remain when the Control of Pollution Act comes into force and replaces most of the relevant provisions of this Act.

The Control of Pollution Act 1974

The system of controls in this Act is similar to that in the existing legislation, but it embodies a more coherent approach, and is more complex.

Waters Subject to Control

Instead of the somewhat piecemeal approach adopted by existing legislation, virtually all waters are brought into the same system. The definition of the various sorts of water are as follows:

Controlled waters

These comprise the sea within three nautical miles from low water mark, such other parts of the territorial sea as are prescribed by regulations, and any other tidal waters in Great Britain. **s56(1)** It should be noted that for the purposes of the Act the area of a water authority includes all the controlled waters off the coast of its area.

Restricted waters

These comprise controlled waters in areas designated as tidal rivers, and other areas where, in the opinion of the Secretary of State, vessels commonly lie at moorings in close proximity to one another. **s56(1)**

Specified underground water

This is underground water in the area of an authority which is used or intended to be used for any purpose and of which prescribed particulars are kept available for public inspection. **s56(1)**

Stream

This is any river, watercourse or inland water, whether natural or artificial, whether above or below ground, except:

(a) A lake, loch or pond which does not discharge into a stream, unless regulations are made specifically to include it in the definition.
(b) A sewer vested in a water authority.
(c) Tidal waters which include an enclosed dock adjoining tidal waters. **s56(1),(3)**

Relevant waters

This is a category upon which much of the Act is based, and is defined as a stream, controlled waters or specified underground water. **s31(1)(a)**

Polluting Matter˙

Offences

It is an offence for any person to cause or knowingly permit:

(a) Any poisonous, noxious or polluting matter to enter any relevant waters.

(b) Any matter to enter a stream which either directly or indirectly, or in combination with other material, tends to impede the proper flow of the water in a manner leading or likely to lead to a substantial aggravation of pollution due to other causes, or of the consequences of such pollution.

(c) Any solid waste to enter a stream or restricted waters. **s31(1)**

Defences and exceptions

The Act contains certain defences and exceptions to the above offences. These are

(1) That the entry in question was authorised by or was a consequence of an act authorised by a disposal licence (see p 66) or a consent given by the Secretary of State or a water authority in pursuance of the Act (see p 32), and that the entry or act was in accordance with the conditions, if any, contained in the licence or consent.

(2) That the entry was authorised by or was a consequence of an act authorised by:

  (i) s34 of the Water Act 1945 which concerned the temporary discharge by water undertakings in connection with the construction of works forming part of their undertaking.

  (ii) Any prescribed enactment.

  (iii) Any provision of a statutory order or local Act which expressly confers power to discharge effluent into water.

  (iv) Any licence granted under the Dumping At Sea Act 1974 (see p 160).

(3) That the entry was attributable to an act or omission which is in accordance with good agricultural practice, unless a notice

to discontinue has been served and the entry occurred twenty-eight days after the service of the notice (see p 44).

(4) That the entry was caused or permitted in an emergency to avoid danger to the public and particulars were given to the water authority as soon as reasonably practicable afterwards.

(5) That the entry was of trade or sewage effluent controlled by s32 (see p 31), and was not from a vessel.

(6) That the entry consists only of permitting water from an abandoned mine to enter relevant waters.

(7) No offence will be committed under Offences (b) and (c) above by reason of the depositing of solid refuse from a mine or quarry so that it falls into a stream or restricted waters, provided that the deposit is made with the consent of the relevant water authority which must not be unreasonably withheld. In addition, there must be no other reasonably practicable site for the deposit of the waste, and all reasonably practicable steps must have been taken to prevent the refuse reaching the water concerned. **s31(2),(3)**

Penalties

Under Offences (a) or (c), the maximum penalties are, on summary conviction, a fine of £400, or three months' imprisonment, or both, and on conviction on indictment, an unlimited fine, or two years' imprisonment, or both. Under Offence (b), the maximum penalty is a fine on summary conviction of £200. **s31(7)**

Discretionary powers

Wide discretionary powers are given to enable regulations to be made to impose further controls over pollution.

They may lay down the precautions to be taken by any person having control or possession of any poisonous, noxious or polluting matter so as to prevent it from entering any relevant waters. The regulations may provide that the contravention is an offence and may prescribe maximum penalties. **s31(4)**

The Secretary of State may also make regulations to prevent poisonous, noxious or polluting matter from entering relevant waters by prohibiting or restricting in a particular area activities which he considers likely to result in water pollution. Such regulations may designate the area, may provide that prescribed activities shall not be carried on within the area except with the consent of the relevant water authority which must not be unreasonably withheld, and may provide that contravention of the regulations is an offence and prescribe maximum penalties. **s31(5)**

In both of the above cases, the maximum penalties which can be imposed for a breach of the regulations are, on summary conviction, a fine of £400, or three months' imprisonment, or both, and on conviction on indictment, an unlimited fine, or two years' imprisonment, or both. The regulations, however, may prescribe smaller sums as the maximum penalties in particular cases. In addition, in the case of a continuing offence punishable on summary conviction, the regulations may impose a maximum fine of £50 per day on which the offence continues after conviction. **s31(7),(8)**

A water authority also has powers to make byelaws prohibiting or regulating the washing or cleaning in any stream or controlled waters in its area of any thing specified in the byelaws. An offender will be liable to a maximum fine on summary conviction of £200, or such smaller sum as may be specified. **s31(6)**

Trade and Sewage Effluent, etc

Offences

It is an offence if any person causes or knowingly permits:

(a) Any trade or sewage effluent to be discharged into any relevant waters from land in Great Britain, through a pipe into the sea outside controlled waters or from a building or from plant, onto or into any land, or into any lake, loch or pond which does not discharge into a stream.

(b) Any matter other than trade or sewage effluent to be discharged into any relevant waters from a sewer or drain.

(c) Any matter other than trade or sewage effluent to be discharged into any relevant waters from a drain which a highway authority or other person is entitled to keep open by virtue of s103 of the Highways Act 1959, provided that the water authority has given at least three months' notice that this provision is to apply to the drain.

Where there is a discharge from works or a sewer of sewage effluent which a water authority did not actually cause or permit, and the authority was bound to receive the effluent either unconditionally or subject to conditions which were observed, then the authority will be deemed to have caused the discharge for the purposes of (a) above.

Defences and exceptions

(a) It will not be an offence if the discharge is made with the consent of the water authority in whose area it occurs, or the Secretary of State, and any conditions in the consent are observed.

(b) The Secretary of State may by order exempt from the provisions of this section any discharge for which consent was not necessary under the 1951 and 1961 Acts or the Water Resources Act 1963, but he can subsequently vary or revoke this order. This power must be exercised before the section comes into force, and is essentially a flexible power to provide for transitional arrangements from the old to the new legislation.

(c) This section does not apply to a discharge from a vessel.

(d) It will be a defence if the discharge is authorised by a licence granted under the Dumping at Sea Act 1974 (see p 160).

(e) It will not be an offence if the discharge was caused or permitted in an emergency to avoid danger to the public, and as soon as reasonably practicable after it had occurred particulars were given to the relevant authority.

(f) A water authority will not be guilty of an offence if there was a discharge from a works or sewer which contravened the conditions of a consent if this was caused by another person making a discharge which the authority was not bound to receive, or which was subject to conditions which were not complied with, and which the authority could not reasonably be expected to have prevented.

(g) It is not an offence if there is a discharge into a sewer or a works vested in a water authority and the authority was bound to receive it either unconditionally or subject to conditions which were observed.

Penalties

The maximum penalties for any of the above offences are, on summary conviction, a fine of £400, or three months' imprisonment, or both, and on conviction on indictment, two years' imprisonment, or an unlimited fine, or both. **s32**

Consents

Central to the scheme of the legislation is the prohibition of unlicensed discharges. As a corollary, a discharge made in accordance with the terms of a consent is no offence. It should be noted that under the 1974 Act there is only provision for consents to discharges. Unlike the old legislation, there is no system of consents to outlets as such. Finally, it should also be noted that under these provisions the consent is to the discharge rather than to a person (cf disposal licences).

Applications for consent

An application for a consent to a discharge must be made to the relevant water authority and must state the following:

(a) The place at which it is proposed to make the discharge.
(b) The nature and composition of the matter to be discharged and its maximum temperature at the time of the discharge.
(c) The maximum quantity which it is proposed to discharge on any one day and the highest rate of discharge.

Once an application has been received, the authority can give its consent unconditionally or subject to conditions, or it can refuse its consent, but consent must not be unreasonably withheld. If within three months from the date of the receipt of the application the authority has not made a decision, then the application will be deemed to have been refused unless either an extension of time has been agreed between the authority and the applicant, or the authority informs the applicant that the application has been referred to the Secretary of State for determination. **s34(1),(2)**

The deliberate or reckless giving of false information in an application for consent is a criminal offence with maximum penalties of a fine of £400 on summary conviction or, on conviction on indictment, two years' imprisonment, or an unlimited fine, or both. **s35(5)**

Unauthorised discharges

Where it appears to a water authority that, without consent, a person has caused or permitted a discharge in contravention of s32 and that a similar contravention is likely, it may serve on that person a written instrument giving consent and may impose such conditions as could have been imposed had there been a proper application. This will not be retrospective, and therefore it does not excuse discharges made before it was given. **s34(3)**

33

Conditions

As has been mentioned, a consent may be given subject to conditions, and it is important to note that a failure to observe the conditions makes the discharge unlicensed and subject to the penalties set out above. For a discharge not to be a criminal offence, it must be made with the consent of the authority and any conditions must have been observed.

The authority may impose such reasonable conditions as it thinks fit, but these must be in accordance with the general scheme and objectives of the Act. The Act does not lay down any standards to be applied by the authority. Rather, in accordance with the general principles of English environmental protection legislation, the Act lays down broad headings, leaving the authority to respond in the light of the particular problems of the locality.

The Act sets out a list of the most common matters which may be covered in conditions. These are:

(a) The places where the discharge will be made and the design and construction of outlets.

(b) The nature, composition, temperature, rate and volume of the discharge, and the periods during which the discharge may be made.

(c) The provision of facilities for the taking of samples of the effluent, in particular the provision, maintenance and use of manholes, inspection chambers, observation wells and boreholes.

(d) The provision, maintenance and testing of meters for measuring the volume and rate of the discharge of the effluent, and apparatus for determining the nature, composition and temperature of the effluent.

(e) The keeping of records of the nature, composition, temperature, volume and rate of the discharge, in particular the keeping of records of the reading of meters and other recording apparatus.

(f) The making of returns and the furnishing of other information to the authority concerning the nature, composition, temperature, volume and rate of the discharge.

(g) The steps to be taken to prevent the discharges from coming into contact with specified underground water.

A consent may be given subject to different conditions for different periods, ie, in phases. **s34(4)**

34

Referral of applications to the Secretary of State

Applications are normally made to a water authority, but there is provision for the Secretary of State to take over this role. If he so decides, either as a result of representations made to him or otherwise, he may direct that a specified application or an application of a specified kind should be transmitted to him for determination. The authority must comply, and must inform the applicant that this has happened. The Secretary of State may in any case, and must if the applicant or the authority requests, hold a public inquiry or give the parties an opportunity to be heard.

If a hearing rather than an inquiry is ordered, the Secretary of State must allow any person who has made representations concerning the application to be heard.

The actual form of the determination is a direction to the authority to refuse its consent, or to give it either unconditionally or subject to such conditions as may be specified in the direction. **s35**

In addition, the Secretary of State may have a further role. Since a water authority is responsible for sewage services, it will, in many cases, require a consent to make a discharge in its own area. Regulations may provide that in this case the consent shall be given by the Secretary of State. **s55**

Publicity of applications

Provisions are introduced by the Act for an increase in publicity concerning applications and consents. The following matters apply both to applications for consent and to instruments giving consent to unauthorised discharges.

Before determining an application or after serving an instrument the authority must publish, in such form as may be laid down, particulars of the application or instrument. The notice must be published for two successive weeks in a newspaper or newspapers circulating in the area where the discharge is made or is proposed to be made, and in areas in the vicinity of a stream or controlled waters which the authority thinks are likely to be affected by the discharge. Not earlier than the day after the first publication has been effected, a similar notice must be published in the London Gazette. Copies of the notice must also be sent to local authorities in whose areas the discharge or proposed discharge is situated. If the application or instrument relates to controlled waters or to the sea outside controlled waters, a copy must also be sent to the Secretary of State and the Minister of Agriculture, Fisheries and

Food. The authority can recover the cost of the notices published in the local newspapers and the London Gazette from the applicant.

The authority must consider any representations made by any person within six weeks beginning with the date on which the notice was published in the London Gazette. If there are representations and after due consideration the authority proposes to give consent to the application, it must serve a notice of its proposed decision on any person who has made them. This notice must contain a statement to the effect that within twenty-one days beginning with the date on which the notice was served, he may, in accordance with regulations, make a request to the Secretary of State asking him to direct that the application should be referred to him for determination. During these twenty-one days the authority cannot finally decide the application. If the applicant has made a request to the Secretary of State and informed the authority, the application cannot be determined unless the Secretary of State gives notice to the authority that he declines to call it in.

The authority can disregard the service of copy notices on local authorities and the publicity requirements if it proposes to give consent to the application and is of the opinion that the discharges will have no appreciable effect on the water into which they will be made. This exemption does not extend to those copies which must be given to the Secretary of State and the Minister of Agriculture, Fisheries and Food.

Where the Secretary of State has directed that an application for consent is to be transferred to him for determination, the provisions as to publicity apply, subject to any modifications which might be made by regulations. **s36(1)–(6)**

Variation and revocation of consents

Water authorities have to make periodical reviews of consents and any conditions attached which they have given. By notice served on the person making the discharge, the authority may revoke the consent if it is reasonable to do so or make reasonable modifications to the existing conditions, or, where the consent is unconditional, impose reasonable conditions.

The Secretary of State has certain powers in this respect. Either as a result of representations received by him or otherwise, he can serve a notice on the authority requiring it to serve a notice of revocation or variation containing such matters as he may direct. If the authority fails to comply with this direction, then the Secretary of State may serve the notice on its behalf. If he does so, for the purposes of the Act, the notice is deemed to have been served by the authority. **s37**

There are certain restrictions on the use of the power to vary or revoke consents, and these apply equally to notices served by an authority and to those served by the Secretary of State in the exercise of his default powers.

Where the authority gives its consent to a discharge, the document containing the consent must specify a reasonable period of not less than two years during which no notice of variation or revocation of that consent will be served without the agreement in writing of the person making the discharge. Similarly, where a notice of variation is served it must also specify a minimum period, again not less than two years, during which no further notice of variation will be served.

There are exceptions to the principle of a minimum period of two years between variations. These are:

(a) The minimum period can be disregarded if the water authority is of the opinion that it is necessary to serve a notice of variation or revocation to protect those who would be likely to be affected by discharges which could be lawfully made were the notice not served, ie, where the observance of the original terms of the consent would not, for some reason, provide adequate protection to the environment.

(b) There is no minimum time limit where the authority gives consent by an instrument to an unauthorised discharge. If, as the result of representations received after the publicity require-ments have been observed (only necessary after the consent has been given), the authority decides that it is appropriate to vary the terms of the consent, it may do so although within two years from the date of the original instrument. **s38(1)–(3)**

Compensation

In some circumstances where a consent is varied or revoked the Act gives a right to compensation, although this is somewhat limited.

No compensation is payable where the variation or revocation takes place in pursuance of the statutory obligations to make a review and is made after the expiry of the minimum period specified.

Compensation is only payable where there has been a variation within the minimum period and there has been no written agree-ment to waive that period. There is an obligation for an authority to pay compensation if the notice is served as a result of a direction by the Secretary of State or if the authority itself serves it, unless in the latter case:

(a) The notice states that in the authority's opinion it is required because of a change in circumstances (including a change in the information relating to the discharges, or relating to the interaction of those discharges with other discharges) which has occurred since the date on which the consent or the earlier variation came into effect, that this could not have been reasonably foreseen and arises otherwise than as a result of consents issued since that date. The notice must also state the reasons for the authority's opinion.

Where a notice containing such a statement is served, the recipient may request the Secretary of State to direct that the notice shall have effect as if the statement were omitted, and if he thinks fit, he may so do. This direction has the effect of removing what would have been a bar to compensation.

(b) The consent was given initially to an unauthorised discharge, and the notice of variation or revocation is served within the period of three months beginning with the date on which the notice of the instrument was published in the London Gazette.

Regulations may be made to provide for the way in which compensation is to be calculated, including factors to be taken into consideration in calculating that figure, and presumably for referring disputes to arbitration. **s38(4),(5)**

Appeals to the Secretary of State

A person who is dissatisfied with an authority's decision may appeal to the Secretary of State. There is no right of appeal where the Secretary of State has determined an application as the result of calling it in.

There can be an appeal to the Secretary of State on whether:

(a) An authority has unreasonably withheld its consent to the deposit of solid waste from a mine or a quarry.
(b) An authority has unreasonably withheld its consent to an application for a consent to make a discharge.
(c) An authority has unreasonably withheld its consent where regulations have been made by the Secretary of State restricting or prohibiting activities in a particular area without consent. It should be noted that if the applicant obtains a certificate from the Minister of Agriculture that the activity in question was

good agricultural practice, any appeal is to be heard jointly by the Secretary of State and the Minister of Agriculture.

(d) An authority when giving its consent to a discharge or to an activity restricted or prohibited by regulations has imposed unreasonable conditions.

(e) A notice of revocation or variation of consent contains terms which are unreasonable, excluding any terms as to the period of time during which there will be no further variation.

(f) The period specified in a consent or a notice of variation during which there will be no variation or revocation is reasonable.

The detailed procedure to be followed with respect to appeals and time limits for bringing appeals will be dealt with in regulations, but certain procedural matters are dealt with in the Act.

Where there is an appeal to the Secretary of State on whether an authority has unreasonably withheld its consent or has given its consent subject to conditions which are unreasonable, and representations concerning the application were made to the authority under the provisions relating to publicity regarding applications, he must ensure that the authority has served notice of the appeal on anyone who made the representations. Before determining the appeal, the Secretary of State must take into consideration any further written representations which might be made to him within a specified period.

Where there is a dispute as to whether the authority has reasonably refused consent or has imposed reasonable conditions, the authority will be treated as having acted reasonably until the contrary is proved. This means that the original decision will be effective until the Secretary of State directs otherwise. The only exception is concerned with the reasonableness of conditions attached to a consent to an activity restricted under regulations, where the consent will be treated as unconditional until the determination of the appeal.

Where there has been an appeal and the Secretary of State decides that the authority has acted unreasonably, he can give a direction to it containing such terms as he thinks appropriate, and the authority must comply with them. **s39**

Transitional provisions

The details of the provisions dealing with the change from the old system to the new will be contained in regulations. Broadly, the position will be as follows:

Existing consents

Regulations will provide that any consent to a discharge and any conditions attached issued under the 1951 and 1961 Acts or the Water Resources Act 1963 will have effect as if issued under the Control of Pollution Act. Since the new system is of consents to discharges only, special provision will be necessary for consents to outlets under the old legislation. Regulations will set out the circumstances in which a consent to an outlet will have effect, with or without modifications, as if it were a consent to a discharge under the 1974 Act.

Pending applications

Where an application for consent has been made under the old legislation and has not been determined, it will take effect as if it were an application for a consent under the 1974 Act made on the day when it was actually made.

Exempt discharges

If (before s32(1) comes into force) an application for consent has been made in respect of a discharge which could lawfully have been made under the old legislation without consent and which is not exempt from the new controls by virtue of regulations made by the Secretary of State, the authority will be treated as having given unconditional consent. For this to apply, the discharge must be substantially a continuation of a discharge made without consent during the year ending 30 April 1974, ignoring any reduction in the temperature, volume or rate of discharge.

This deemed unconditional consent lasts until either the authority gives its actual unconditional consent or, where it refuses consent or gives it subject to conditions, until the end of three months from the date on which notice of the decision was served on the applicant. If during this period the applicant appeals to the Secretary of State, the unconditional consent lasts until the determination of the appeal.

Pending appeals

Regulations will provide that any appeal pending under the 1951 or 1961 Acts or the Water Resources Act 1963 will be treated as an appeal under the 1974 Act. **s40**

Registers

Water authorities must keep a register containing particulars of various matters, details of which will be contained in regulations. These are:

(a) Applications for consents to discharges.
(b) Consents given, and the conditions attached, except deemed unconditional consents under the transitional provisions.
(c) Samples of effluent obtained under s113 of the Water Resources Act, samples of water taken, information produced from the analysis of such samples, and the steps taken as the result of the information.
(d) Certificates of exemption issued by the Secretary of State (see below).
(e) Copies of notices to abstain from certain agricultural practices which have been served on the authority, other than notices of rejections of applications (see p 44).

These registers are to be open to public inspection, free of charge, at all reasonable hours, and on payment of a reasonable charge the public are to be allowed to obtain copies of entries.

These provisions are much wider than those concerned with registers under the old legislation, whereby the only persons allowed to inspect them were those interested in the land, premises or outlet from which the effluent was discharged, or persons authorised by them. **s41**

Restrictions on Publicity

The principle that the public are entitled to increased information on pollution and associated matters is embodied in the provisions regarding publicity and the register. In certain circumstances, however, a limited right of exemption from publicity is conferred.

A person who has applied or intends to apply to a water authority for a consent to a discharge may apply to the Secretary of State for a certificate exempting the application and any consent, and any sample and information derived from the analysis of such a sample, from the publicity requirements for applications and registers. The applicant must satisfy the Secretary of State that publicity would either prejudice to an unreasonable extent some private interest by disclosing information about a trade secret, or would be contrary to the public interest. If the Secretary of State is so satisfied, he may, but need not, issue a certificate providing that the publicity requirements shall not apply to such matters as may be specified in the certificate.

If a person is making or proposes to make a discharge which is the subject of a consent under the old legislation and therefore subject to a very limited degree of disclosure, he may apply to the Secretary of State for a certificate of exemption. The grounds of exemption and the procedure are the same as in respect of an application under the 1974 Act.

It should be noted that particulars of this certificate must be contained in the register, and it is not possible to claim an exemption from this requirement. **s42**

Powers to Remedy Pollution

Under the Water Resources Act, water authorities had powers to act in emergencies to remedy pollution caused by an accident or other unforeseen event. These are replaced by much wider powers under the 1974 Act.

(a) If it appears to an authority that pollution injurious to plant or animal life in a stream in its area has occurred as a result of discharges made under a consent given or varied by it, then it must exercise its powers to vary or revoke the consent to ensure that further similar discharges are not made. The person making the discharge must be given such period as the authority considers necessary in which to ensure that such discharges are not made or, where the consent is revoked, to discontinue the discharge. During this time the authority must take appropriate action as soon as is reasonably practicable to remedy or mitigate the effect of the pollution. At the end of this period the authority must take all necessary steps to restore the plant and animal life of the stream to the condition in which they were before the discharge was made.

Where pollution has been caused by a discharge, but, in the opinion of the authority, after a reasonable time and after steps have been taken to restore the plant and animal life, injurious pollution will not be caused by its continuance, it is not obliged to revoke or modify the consent. However, in these circumstances it must take action to remedy and mitigate the effects of the pollution and take steps to restore the plant and animal life of the stream.

If an authority is exercising these powers, no account is to be taken of any minimum period specified in the consent or prior notice of variation within which there will be no variation.

However, if a consent is varied, compensation will be payable by the authority if the requirements under Variation and Revocation of Consents (p 37) are met. In this situation an authority must exercise its powers even though in doing so it makes itself liable to pay compensation. **s46(1)–(3)**

(b) Where it appears to an authority that any solid waste or poisonous, noxious or polluting matter is likely to enter, or is or has been present in any relevant waters in its area, it may carry out either there or elsewhere such operations as it considers appropriate to prevent those substances entering the waters, to remove or dispose of them, to remedy any pollutant effects and to restore the waters to the condition they were in before the pollution occurred. However, in exercising these powers an authority is not entitled to impede or prevent the making of a discharge which is authorised by a consent. **s46(4)**

(c) Where an authority carries out operations under the above powers, it can recover the costs from the person who made the polluting discharge or who caused the polluting matter to enter the waters, or to be so situated as to be likely to enter the waters.

No costs will be payable by such a person if he can establish to the satisfaction of the court in which the authority is trying to recover them that they were incurred unnecessarily. Costs are not payable if the matter in question is water from an abandoned mine, nor if the person is entitled to compensation for the variation of a consent. **s46(5),(6)**

Cleansing of Stream Beds

It is an offence, without the consent of the authority which must not be unreasonably withheld, to remove from any part of the channel or bed of a stream a deposit accumulated by reason of a weir, dam or sluice by causing the deposit to be carried away in suspension in the water of the stream, unless it is done in the exercise of statutory powers conferred by or under an Act relating to land drainage, flood prevention or navigation.

It is also an offence, without consent, to cut or uproot a substantial amount of vegetation in a stream, or so near a stream that it falls in, and to allow that vegetation to remain in the stream.

Any question as to whether the authority's consent has been unreasonably withheld can be referred to the Secretary of State for determination. The maximum penalty for both of these offences on summary conviction is a fine of £200. These provisions may be extended by regulations to specified controlled waters. They are very similar to those under the old legislation, and a consent given under it will be treated as having been given under the 1974 Act. **s49**

Abandoned Mines

A water authority has powers to carry out studies to ascertain what problems relating to the pollution of relevant waters have arisen as the result of the abandonment of a mine in its area, or might arise if it were abandoned. The authority must also find out what steps would be appropriate to deal with these problems, and their costs. Although permitting water from an abandoned mine to pass into relevant waters is not an offence, authorities do have powers of remedial action to deal with such problems under the 'Powers to Remedy Pollution' (b) above, although no costs will be recoverable in respect of such action. **s50**

Good Agricultural Practice

It will be a defence to a charge of polluting relevant waters under s31 if it was done in accordance with good agricultural practice, unless a notice of discontinuance has been served.

The definition of good agricultural practice is 'Any practice recommended in a code of practice approved by the Minister of Agriculture, Fisheries and Food will be deemed to be good agricultural practice, but without prejudice to any evidence that some other practice, not defined in a code of practice, is also good agricultural practice'.

If a water authority is of the opinion that any relevant waters have been or are likely to be polluted as the result of an act or omission in accordance with good agricultural practice, it can apply in writing to the Secretary of State requesting him to serve a notice on the occupier of the land in question requiring him to prevent such acts or omissions.

The application must specify the acts or omissions, and the authority's reason for its opinion. A copy of it must be served on the Minister of Agriculture, Fisheries and Food, and on the occupier of the land. The occupier must also be served with a statement informing him that he has a right to make written representations to the Secretary of State within twenty-eight days from the date on which the notice was served on him.

After considering any such representations, the Secretary of State must serve the occupier with a notice of his decision, and send the authority a copy of it. This may comply with the terms of the authority's request, include less restrictive terms or state that the application has been rejected.

An authority must keep in its register details of copies of such notices from the Secretary of State, except for those which reject applications, together with the dates of service on them.

If the Secretary of State considers that a notice should be cancelled he must inform the authority and consider any representations it may make. He may then serve a notice on the occupier of the land, stating that the original notice has been cancelled. A copy of the notice of cancellation must be served on the authority, and it must enter a statement on the register that the notice is or will be, at a specified time, cancelled. **s51**

Sanitary Appliances on Vessels

Water authorities are given powers to regulate the use of sanitary appliances on vessels. In general, this means that since 1 January 1979 it has been an offence to use a sanitary appliance on board a vessel on a stream or in restricted waters if it is not sealed in such a way as to prevent material passing from the vessel into water. **s33**

Since sanitary appliances can no longer discharge into waters, some alternative provision must be made for the disposal of their contents. Water authorities must make arrangements for the collection and disposal of waste from vessels, and provide facilities for washing out these appliances. An authority, in order to minimise pollution, may also provide toilets and washing facilities for the use of people from vessels. **s47**

To prevent pollution, the authority may make byelaws prohibiting vessels from being on specified streams in its area unless they are registered with the authority or exempt from registration under the byelaws.

Contravention of such a byelaw can be punished with a maximum penalty on summary conviction of a £50 fine. The authority may make reasonable charge for registration, and the implication is that the registration fees will finance the use of the facilities, since no charge is payable by persons from a registered vessel. **s48**

Charges

Under the Water Act 1973, a water authority can fix charges in respect of services performed or facilities provided. These may be detailed in a charges scheme which must show the methods of calculating them, and be given adequate publicity. These charging powers may be extended to discharges regulated by consents under the 1974 Act if the Secretary of State, after consultation with the National Water Council, makes an order to that effect. If the order so provides, but not otherwise, the authority need not take into account the actual cost of the services performed or facilities provided when fixing charges. This order must also contain provision for appeals to the Secretary of State in respect of charges payable to a water authority, and it may be revoked or varied by a subsequent order.

An order under this provision requires an affirmative resolution of both Houses of Parliament, unlike most orders to be made under the Act which take effect unless Parliament resolves to the contrary. **s52**

Enforcement

The provisions of the Control of Pollution Act 1974 are available to enforce these controls. (see p 156).

B.   DISPOSAL OF LIQUID WASTE

The above legislation deals with the system of controls imposed on the discharge of effluents into rivers, streams and coastal waters, and the regulation of activities which could directly cause pollution. It applies equally to private persons and public bodies, and to the disposal by water authorities of both industrial and sewage effluent.

The discharge of effluent into the public sewage system prior to the discharge into water is regulated by different legislation, although the broad effect is similar.

The relevant legislation is the Public Health Acts of 1936 and 1961, the Public Health (Drainage of Trade Premises) Act 1937 and several provisions of the Control of Pollution Act 1974.

The responsibilities for administering the legislation were placed originally on local authorities, but under the Water Act 1973 they were transferred to the various regional water authorities.

The Public Health Act 1936

Water authorities have a duty to provide such public sewers as are necessary for the effectual drainage of their districts and to make

46

arrangements for the treatment of sewage. Certain matters are not allowed to enter public sewers:

(a) Any matter likely to injure any sewer or drain or to interfere with the free flow of the contents or to affect prejudicially the treatment and disposal of the contents.
(b) Any chemical refuse or waste steam, or any liquid with a temperature of over 110°F which either alone or in combination with other matters is a nuisance or prejudicial to health.
(c) Any petroleum spirit or calcium carbide. s27/36
(d) No person is to discharge either directly or indirectly into a public sewer any liquid from a factory other than domestic sewage or surface or storm water, or any liquid from any manufacturing process, or any other matter which is prohibited from entering the sewer under any enactment. s34/36

Under this Act, an authority is not permitted to use a sewer or a drain or outfall to conduct foul water to a natural or artificial stream or other body of water until that water has been so treated as not to affect prejudicially the purity and quality of the water into which it is discharged.

Thus, under the 1936 Act an authority must receive certain effluents into its sewers and must treat them before they are discharged into waters for disposal, and industrial effluents may not be discharged into public sewers. The position regarding trade effluents is regulated by the 1937 Act as amended.

Trade Effluent Legislation

Definition of Trade Effluents

Trade effluents are liquids with or without particles in suspension produced wholly or partly in the course of a trade or industry carried on at trade premises. Domestic sewage is specifically excluded from the definition since this, even if produced at trade premises, comes under the general scheme of the 1936 Act. s14/37

The basic provision of the 1937 Act is that notwithstanding any restriction in the 1936 Act, trade effluents, with the consent of the water authority, may be discharged into the public sewers. The only restriction now remaining is that petroleum and calcium carbide are also prohibited under the trade effluent legislation.

Under the 1961 Act, the definition of trade or industry was extended to include agriculture, horticulture, and scientific research and experiment. Effluents from premises used for these purposes thus became trade effluents and subject to the Act. **s63/61**

Trade Effluent Notices: Consents and Conditions

The discharge of trade effluents into public sewers is permitted, provided the consent of the water authority has been obtained. No trade effluent may be discharged into a public sewer except in accordance with the terms of a trade effluent notice which has been served on the water authority. This notice must state:

(a) The nature and composition of the effluent.
(b) The maximum daily quantity of the effluent to be discharged.
(c) The maximum rate of discharge.

No effluent may be discharged in accordance with such a notice until the expiry of two months from the date on which the notice is served on the authority, or such lesser period as may be agreed. This is the initial period.

A trade effluent notice is to be treated as an application for the authority's consent. **s2(1), (2)/37**

At any time during the initial period the authority may give the occupier of the premises a direction that no trade effluent is to be discharged until a specified date after the initial period expires. If, after such a direction has been given, it appears to the authority that as the result of a failure to complete any works for the reception and disposal of the trade effluent or as the result of some other exceptional circumstances, a later date than that specified in the direction is necessary, it may apply to the Secretary of State who can extend (or curtail) the period during which effluent may not be discharged. An authority must give the owner and occupier of the trade premises concerned at least one month's notice of its intention to apply, and the Secretary of State must consider any representations made. **s2(3)/37;s62/61**

In dealing with the trade effluent notice, the authority may refuse its consent or may give its consent either unconditionally or subject to conditions concerning the following matters:

(a) The sewer or sewers into which the effluent may be discharged.
(b) The nature or composition of the effluent.
(c) The maximum quantity which may be discharged on one day, either generally or into a particular sewer.
(d) The highest rate at which effluent may be discharged, either generally or into a particular sewer.

(e) The period or periods of the day during which the trade effluent may be discharged into the sewer.

(f) The exclusion from the effluent of all condensing water.

(g) The elimination or diminution of any specified constituent of the effluent before it enters the sewer if the authority believes that that substance either alone or in combination with any matter with which it may come into contact while in the sewer would injure or obstruct the sewer, or make the treatment or disposal of the sewage especially difficult or expensive or, where the sewage is to be discharged into a harbour or tidal waters, would adversely affect navigation in the harbour or tidal waters or their use.

(h) The temperature of the effluent at the time of its discharge into the sewer, and its acidity or alkalinity at that time.

(i) The payment of charges for the reception and disposal of the effluent having regard to the nature, composition, volume and rate of discharge, any additional expense incurred by the authority in connection with the reception and disposal of the effluent, and any revenue likely to be derived from it.

(j) The provision and maintenance of an inspection chamber or manhole, etc, to enable samples to be taken at any time of the effluent passing into the sewer.

(k) The provision of meters to measure the volume and rate of discharge into the sewer, and the testing of such meters.

(l) The provision of apparatus for determining the nature and composition of any trade effluent passing into the sewer, and the testing of such apparatus.

(m) The keeping of records of the volume, the rate of discharge, the nature and composition of any effluent and in particular, the keeping of records of the readings of meters required under another condition.

(n) The making of returns, and the giving of other information to the authority concerning the volume, rate of discharge, composition and nature of the effluent. **s2(3)/37, s59/61**

Penalties

If trade effluent is discharged without consent, or any conditions imposed in a consent are not complied with, the occupier of the premises from which the discharge was made will be guilty of an offence and liable on summary conviction to a maximum penalty of a fine of £200 and, in addition, a further fine of £50 for every day on which the offence continues after conviction. **s2(5)/37**

Variation of Conditions

The provisions concerning variation of conditions are very similar to those for consents to discharges from streams.

A water authority has a power to vary the conditions contained in a consent by giving a direction to that effect. Notice of the direction must be given to the owner or occupier of the premises from which the discharge is made. It must contain a statement that he has a right to appeal to the Secretary of State against the direction within the period of two months from the date when the notice was served on him, or such longer period as the authority may agree. It must specify the date on which the variation will take effect and this must be not less than two months from the giving of the notice. However, where the variation relates to the payment of charges, that variation can take effect at any time after the giving of the notice. If there is an appeal, the variation will not take effect until it is withdrawn or finally disposed of.

Where there is an appeal, the Secretary of State may annul the direction or substitute for it another variation either more or less favourable to the appellant, and any direction he makes may include provisions as to the charges to be made in respect of any period between the giving of the notice and the determination of the appeal.

An authority may not, except as is provided below, give a direction varying the terms of a consent within the period of two years from the date of the consent or the date of the giving of a previous direction, without the written consent of the owner and occupier of the trade premises concerned. **s60/61**

Such a direction may be given within that period and without consent if the authority considers it necessary to do so in order to provide proper protection for persons likely to be affected by discharges which could otherwise be lawfully made.

Compensation

In the event of an early variation there is a right to compensation similar to that given in respect of discharges to streams. An authority will have to pay compensation unless it is of the opinion that the direction is required because of a change of circumstances (including the information available concerning the discharge or its interaction with other discharges or matter) which has occurred since the beginning of the two-year period, and could not then have been reasonably foreseen, and the direction is required otherwise than as the result of consents to discharges given after the beginning of that period. The authority must give a statement of its reasons to the owner and occupier of the property.

A person who receives this notice may appeal to the Secretary of State in accordance with regulations on the grounds that compensation should be payable. On appeal, the Secretary of State may direct that the statement of reasons which must be given by the authority is to be ignored for the purpose of compensation, thus removing a bar to payment. Any regulations made concerning the provision of compensation for an early variation of consents to discharges to streams shall apply equally under this provision. **s45/74**

Appeals to the Secretary of State

In addition to the above, there is a general right of appeal. A person may appeal to the Secretary of State against:

(a) A direction by an authority that no discharge may be made under a trade effluent notice until a specified date after the end of the initial period.
(b) The refusal of an authority to give consent.
(c) The failure of an authority to give consent within the initial period.
(d) Any condition attached to a consent.

Where there is an appeal under (a), the Secretary of State may vary the direction by substituting an earlier or later date than that specified in the direction. Where there is an appeal under (b) or (c), he may give consent either unconditionally or subject to such conditions as he thinks fit having regard to matters which can be covered by conditions which may be imposed by an authority.

Where there is an appeal under (d), the Secretary of State may review all the conditions attached to the consent including those not appealed against, and may substitute any other set of conditions, whether more or less favourable to the appellant, or he may annul any of the conditions.

Where there is an appeal on any of the above grounds, in addition to refusing the appeal, he may direct that no trade effluent shall be discharged in accordance with the trade effluent notice until a specified date.

Where there is an appeal concerning a condition relating to charges, the Secretary of State may include provisions as to the charges to be payable for any period before the determination of the appeal. **s3/37, s61/61**

Trade Effluent Agreements

A water authority may enter into trade effluent agreements with the owner or occupier of any trade premises in its area for the reception and disposal of any trade effluent produced on the premises. In particular, the agreement may provide for the authority to construct such works as may be necessary for its reception and disposal, and for the repayment by the owner or occupier of all or part of the expenses incurred by the authority in carrying out its obligations under the agreement.

An authority may also enter into an agreement to remove and dispose of substances produced in the course of treating trade effluent on or in connection with the premises. A copy of any such agreement must be kept available for public inspection. **s7/37**

Exempt Discharges

Under the 1937 Act, certain discharges were exempt from the controls, but the Control of Pollution Act removes these exemptions. The two categories which were exempt were those which were substantially a continuance of discharges lawfully made during the year ending 3 March 1937 and discharges made under a trade effluent agreement entered into before that date.

The exemptions are removed in the case of pre-1937 discharges and pre-1937 agreements which do not contain an express provision whereby the authority can terminate the agreement, whether or not there has been a breach. (Where this express provision exists, there is no need for a statute to allow the termination of the agreement since the authority may do this under the terms of the agreement.)

A person making a discharge in either of these two categories immediately before the passing of the Act on 31 July 1974, could have given notice to the authority within six months of that date that such a discharge was so authorised. On 19 July 1976, the day when the section came into force, consent would have been deemed to have been given, and this would have been subject to any conditions imposed under the 1961 Act or contained in the agreement. (Although these discharges were exempt from control under the 1937 Act, the 1961 Act empowered authorities to impose conditions covering matters such as the composition and volume of the effluent, and provision for inspection and monitoring.)

At any time after 19 July 1976, the authority may, and, if so requested by the person making the discharge, must, cancel the deemed consent and give its actual consent. This actual consent may be given unconditionally or subject to the conditions an authority normally has power to impose. The notice giving the actual consent must also contain a statement that the recipient has a right of appeal to the Secretary of State. On an appeal the Secretary of State may make such direction as he thinks fit, and the authority must comply with it. **s43/74**

Details of the appeal procedure are contained in the Control of Pollution (Discharges into Sewers) Regulations 1976 (SI 1976 No 958). Notice of appeal must be given in writing to the Secretary of State within two months from the date of receipt of the notice, or such longer period as may be agreed with the water authority. It must contain a statement of the grounds of appeal, and the following must be forwarded to the Secretary of State:

(a) The notice, and any relevant maps or plans relating to the deemed consent.

(b) The notice giving the actual consent, specifying any conditions to which the actual consent is subject.

(c) All other relevant correspondence with the authority.

A copy of the notice of appeal and the grounds of appeal must be sent to the water authority.

Miscellaneous Provisions

Production of information

The owner or occupier of any premises on or under which is situated a drain or sewer used or intended to be used for discharging any trade effluent to a sewer must, if requested by the authority, produce all such plans, etc, of the drain which he has or can obtain without incurring expense, and allow the authority to have copies made. He must also furnish such information in respect of the drain or sewer as may be reasonably expected of him. Failure to comply with such a request is an offence carrying a maximum penalty on summary conviction of a fine of £50 and a further fine of £5 per day on which the offence continues after conviction. **s9/37**

Samples

Where an officer of the authority exercises his power of entry (see p 151), he may obtain and take away a sample of the effluent passing from the premises to a public sewer. An analysis of this sample will only be admissible in legal proceedings if the occupier is notified as soon as it is taken that it is intended to have it analysed, and there and then the sample is divided into three parts, placed in a suitable container, and sealed. One part must be given to the occupier, one must be retained for future comparison, and the third submitted for analysis. **s10/37**

Extension of controls

Mention has been made of the extension of the Act to agricultural and scientific premises. In addition, the Secretary of State has a power to extend the controls by order to other specified effluents, with any necessary modifications and provision for transitional arrangements. **s64/61**

Recording and testing of effluents

Any meter or other apparatus provided for measuring or testing effluent will be presumed to be accurate until the contrary is proved. The power of entry conferred by the 1936 Act (see p 151) may be exercised for the purpose of reading a meter provided in pursuance of this legislation. **s67/61**

Disclosure of information

Any person who discloses information furnished to him under this legislation will be guilty of an offence unless:

(a) It was done with the consent of the person who furnished it.
(b) It was done in connection with the execution of the legislation.
(c) It was done for the purposes of any proceedings, including an appeal or application to the Secretary of State, arbitration, criminal proceedings, or a report of such proceedings.

The maximum penalties for a contravention of this provision are, on summary conviction, a fine of £100, or three months' imprisonment, or both. **s68/61**

Charges

The provisions whereby the charging provisions of the Water Act 1973 may be extended to the functions of water authorities concerning water pollution apply equally to their functions under the trade effluent legislation. **s52/74**

Enforcement

The enforcement machinery of the Public Health Act 1936 is available to water authorities to enforce trade effluent legislation (see p 151).

CHAPTER THREE

THE DISPOSAL OF WASTE ON LAND

The aspects of common law most relevant to disposal of waste on land are trespass, nuisance, negligence and the Rule in Rylands *v* Fletcher, although each of these torts has its own, often severe limitations (see Chapter 1).

The main piece of legislation was the Public Health Act 1936 which made local authorities responsible for the free collection of house refuse in their areas. After 1974 the responsible authorities became district councils. They also had powers to collect trade refuse, but had to make a reasonable charge for this service. Disputes as to the definition of trade refuse or the reasonableness of charges were to be decided by a court of summary jurisdiction. Local authorities were given powers to provide sites for the deposit of refuse and plant and machinery for its treatment, and to sell refuse. It should also be noted that s92 made 'accumulations or deposits which are prejudicial to health or a nuisance' subject to the statutory nuisance procedure (see p 15).

Other relevant legislation was that controlling litter, and the Civic Amenities Act 1967 which obliged local authorities to provide sites where people could dispose of refuse other than that arising in the course of a business, free of charge. It also gave them powers concerning the dumping of abandoned vehicles and other matter on highways.

In addition, under the Public Health Act 1961 they had powers to remove rubbish deposited on land in their areas which was seriously detrimental to the amenities of the neighbourhood.

This was virtually the sum of the legal provisions relating to the control of waste disposal until the early 1970s. During the 1960s there was increasing disquiet over the problems of the disposal of waste and, in particular, toxic waste. As a result the Committee on the Disposal of Solid Toxic Wastes was appointed, and this body reported in 1970. One of its main recommendations was that the disposal of toxic wastes should be subject to a regulatory procedure, that is, disposal should require the consent of a licensing body, and it recommended that this should be the local authority.

The Deposit of Poisonous Waste Act, passed in 1972, made the depositing of poisonous, noxious or polluting waste on land where its presence would be likely to give rise to an environmental hazard, a criminal offence.

The Act did not introduce a system of licensing, but it did introduce a system requiring notices of the intended deposit of waste to be given to local authorities and river/water authorities.

Most of the above was repealed by the Control of Pollution Act 1974 which is here examined in detail. At the time of writing, most of the relevant sections have been brought into force.

A.   DEPOSIT OF WASTE ON LAND

Disposal Provisions of the Control of Pollution Act 1974

Definitions

Certain terms on which the controls in the Act are based must first be defined.

The Act imposes obligations on local authorities, but not on local authorities as such. Instead, they are classified as disposal and collection authorities.

Disposal authorities

In England these are county councils and the Greater London Council. In Wales they are district councils.

Collection authorities

These are district councils, the London boroughs, the Common Council of the City of London, the Sub-Treasurer of the Inner Temple, and the Under Treasurer of the Middle Temple. **s30(1)**

Waste

Waste includes any substance which constitutes a scrap material, or an effluent, or other unwanted surplus substance arising from the application of a process, and any substance or article which requires to be disposed of as being broken, worn out, contaminated or otherwise spoiled. Explosives are specifically excluded.

There is also a presumption in the Act that anything which is discarded or dealt with as if it were waste will be presumed to be waste unless the contrary is proved.

Waste is divided into three categories:

Household waste: waste from a private dwelling or residential home, or from premises forming part of a hospital or nursing home, or from premises forming part of a school, university or other educational establishment.

Industrial waste: waste from a factory within the meaning of the Factories Act 1961 and from any premises occupied by a body corporate established by or under any enactment for the purpose of carrying on under national ownership any industry or part of an industry or undertaking, but excluding waste from a mine or quarry.

Commercial waste: waste from premises used wholly or mainly for the purposes of a trade or business, or for the purpose of sport, recreation or entertainment, but excluding household and industrial waste, waste from mines and quarries, and waste from agricultural premises.

Regulations may be made to provide that waste of a prescribed description shall or shall not, as the case may be, be treated as falling within one or other of the three categories mentioned above. However, such regulations cannot bring into the scope of the Act waste from mines, quarries, or agricultural premises. Waste does not include sewage or radioactive materials unless regulations specifically provide that the Act shall apply to them. **s30(3)–(5)**

Under the Control of Pollution (Licensing of Waste Disposal) Regulations 1976 (SI 1976 No 732, para 3), waste produced on a building site or as the result of dredging, and sewage deposited on land are to be treated as industrial waste, with certain exceptions. These exceptions were added to by the Control of Pollution (Licensing of Waste Disposal Amendment) Regulations 1977 (SI 1977 No 1185).

The final definition, and one on which much of the scheme of the Act is based, is that of 'controlled waste', that is, household, industrial or commercial waste. **s30(1)**

Basic Duty of Disposal Authority

It is the duty of each disposal authority to ensure that the arrangements made by it and others are adequate for the purpose of disposing of all of the controlled waste which is or is likely to be situated in its area. **s1**

Waste Disposal Plan

Each disposal authority has a duty to carry out an investigation to ascertain what arrangements are needed to dispose of controlled waste which is or is likely to be situated in its area, and then to decide what measures should be taken.

It must next prepare a waste disposal plan, hereafter called 'the plan'. This is a statement of the arrangements which either have been made or are proposed to be made by the authority and other persons for the disposal of waste during a specified period.

After the plan has been made the authority must make periodical reviews to decide what alterations are necessary, and it must make any necessary alterations resulting from the review.

In considering the arrangements to be included in the original plan, or any modification, the authority must have regard to the effect which these would have on the amenities of any relevant locality, and their likely cost to the authority. **s2(1)**

For more details on the preparation of waste disposal plans, see Waste Management Paper No 3: *Guideline for the preparation of a waste disposal plan* (HMSO).

Contents of the plan

Information which must be contained in the plan is as follows:

(a) The kinds and quantities of controlled waste which the authority expects to be situated in its area during the period specified in the plan.
(b) The kinds and quantities of controlled waste which the authority expects to be brought into its area, or taken from it, for the purposes of disposal, during that period.
(c) The kinds and quantities of controlled waste which the authority expects to dispose of itself during that period.
(d) The kinds and quantities of controlled waste which will be disposed of in its area by persons other than the authority during that period.

(e) The methods which the authority considers should be adopted for the disposal of controlled waste in its area, either by reclamation or otherwise, and the priorities which should be accorded to the various methods of disposal.

(f) The sites and equipment which the authority and other persons are providing, or propose to provide, for the purposes of disposing of controlled waste.

(g) The estimated costs of the various methods of disposal mentioned in the plan.

This basic list may be modified by regulations requiring a disposal authority to take into account prescribed matters when preparing the plan or any modification. **s2(2)**

Consultation and publicity

In preparing the plan and any modification to it, a disposal authority must consult the following bodies:

(1) Any water authority, any part of whose area is included in the area of the disposal authority.

(2) Where the plan is prepared by an English disposal authority, the collection authorities whose areas are included in the area of the disposal authority.

(3) Where the plan is prepared by a Welsh disposal authority, the county council in whose area the area of the disposal authority is situated.

(4) Where the plan or modification involves the transport of waste to the area of another disposal authority, that other authority.

(5) In any case, such persons as the authority considers appropriate who are engaged commercially in the disposal of waste or their representatives, and such other persons as may be prescribed.

Before finally determining the plan, the authority must publicise the proposals and take into account any representations which might be made by members of the public, and make such alterations as it considers appropriate.

This requirement of publicity may be dispensed with if the authority is merely making a modification to the plan and it considers that no person will be prejudiced if these requirements are disregarded.

Specific consideration must be given in the preparation of a plan or modification to the question of reclamation. The authority must consult any person it considers appropriate and who agrees, and in England, the collection authorities whose areas are included in the disposal authority's area, as to what arrangements could reasonably be made for the purpose of reclaiming substances from controlled waste, and what provisions should be included in the plan for that purpose.

This requirement can be disregarded where there is a modification of a plan where reclamation is not relevant.

Once this procedure has been completed and the authority has finally determined the content of the plan or modification, it must take such steps as it considers appropriate to give adequate publicity to its contents in its area, and send a copy to the Secretary of State.

Disposal plans do not have to be approved by the Secretary of State but he does have two important functions. If the authority proposes to move waste from its area to another disposal authority's area, the plan cannot be finally determined until that other authority consents. If the other authority refuses its consent, the plan can only be finalised if the Secretary of State consents, thus overriding its objection. Secondly, the Secretary of State can issue a direction to an authority specifying a period within which the authority must carry out any duty imposed on it by the above provisions. **s2(3)-(7)**

Deposit of Waste

One of the major innovations introduced by the Act is the system of licensing of deposits of waste. The corollary of a system of licensing is that compliance with the terms of a licence is a defence to what would otherwise be a criminal offence. It is proposed to examine the offences and ancillary matters first, and then to look at the question of licensing in detail.

Offences

Except in prescribed cases (see below), it is an offence to:

(a) Deposit controlled waste on land or cause or knowingly permit any controlled waste to be so deposited.

(b) Use any plant or equipment, or cause or knowingly permit any plant or equipment to be used for the purpose of disposing of any controlled waste, or of dealing with it in a prescribed manner. **s3(1)**

Penalties

There are two sets of penalties set out in the Act for the above offences which, by implication, create two sets of offences, the deposit of toxic, and the deposit of non-toxic waste.

If there has been a deposit of waste on land, and:

(1) the waste is poisonous, noxious or polluting;
(2) its presence on the land is likely to give rise to an environmental hazard;
(3) the circumstances are such that the person who deposited it can reasonably be assumed to have abandoned it for the purpose of its being disposed of;

the maximum penalties which can be imposed are, on summary conviction, a fine of £400 or six months' imprisonment, or both, or, on conviction on indictment, an unlimited fine, or five years' imprisonment, or both. **s3(3)**

In any other case the maximum penalties are, on summary conviction, a fine of £400, and on conviction on indictment, an unlimited fine, or two years' imprisonment, or both. **s3(2)**

The presence of waste on land gives rise to an environmental hazard if it is deposited or disposed of in such manner and in such quantity that, either by itself or cumulatively with deposits of the same or other substances, it subjects persons or animals to a material risk of death, injury or impairment of health, or threatens the pollution, whether on the surface or underground, of any water supply.

In assessing this risk, the fact that waste is deposited in containers does not of itself exclude any risk which might arise were the waste not in them. Regard must also be had as to the measures, if any, taken by the person depositing the waste, or by the owner or occupier of the land or others, for minimising the risk, and the likelihood of the waste or any containers in which it is deposited being tampered with by children and others. **s4(5),(6)**

Defences

(a) The most important defence is that the waste was deposited on land, or the plant or equipment was situated on land which was occupied by the holder of a disposal licence issued under s5, and which authorised the deposit or use in question, and that the deposit or use was in accordance with the terms of the licence. Thus, a failure to observe the terms of a licence removes this defence, and makes the deposit unlicensed. **s3(1)**

(b) It is a defence if the defendant can prove that he took care to find out from someone in a position to know whether the deposit or use was in contravention of the Act, and had no reason to suppose that the information given was false and that the deposit or use would be in contravention of the Act.

(c) It is a defence for a person charged to prove that he was acting under the instructions of his employer, and had no reason to know or suspect that the use or deposit would be in contravention of the Act.

(d) Where the offence consists of a failure to observe the terms of a licence, it is a defence to prove that all reasonable steps were taken to ensure that conditions in the licence were observed.

(e) It is a defence to prove that the acts specified in the charge were done in an emergency in order to avoid a danger to the public and that, as soon as was reasonably practicable, particulars of the acts were given to the disposal authority in whose area the acts were committed. **s3(4)**

Transitional provisions

Where an activity for which a disposal licence is required was carried on for the period of six months immediately preceding 14 June 1976, when s3 came into force, the prohibitions in s3 did not apply to that activity for the period of one year from that date in order that a disposal licence might be obtained. If at the end of that period an appeal against a refusal to issue a licence or against conditions imposed was pending, the exemption continued until the appeal was determined. **s4(1)**

Exemptions from s3

s3 does not apply to household waste from a private dwelling which is deposited, disposed of, or otherwise dealt with within the curtilage of the dwelling by or with the permission of the occupier. **s4(2)**

This is the only specific exemption contained in the Act, but the Secretary of State is empowered to make regulations to prescribe excepted cases and to exempt certain categories of waste from the controls of s3, and may make different provision for different areas. In deciding whether or not to exempt certain cases, he must have regard to the expediency of exempting from control:

(a) Any deposits which are so small or of such a temporary nature that they can be properly excluded from control.

(b) Any uses of plant or equipment which are so innocuous as to be able to be excluded.

(c) Cases for which adequate controls are provided under other legislation. **s4(3)**

This power to exempt certain cases has been exercised and the excepted cases are contained in the Control of Pollution (Licensing of Waste Disposal) Regulations 1976, (SI 1976 No 732, para 4). It should be noted at the outset that the exemptions do not apply to the deposit or disposal on land or in a receptacle of any substance which is poisonous, noxious or polluting, or of which the presence on the land or in the receptacle is likely to give rise to an environmental hazard. The exemptions can be summarised as follows:

(1) Waste produced in the course of construction or demolition works which is deposited or disposed of on a construction site, provided the deposit or disposal is made with the consent of the occupier of the site.

(2) Waste ash which is deposited on a construction site, again with the consent of the occupier of the site.

(3) Waste produced in the demolition of a building which is deposited on the site of such a demolition.

(4) Spent railway ballast which is deposited on operational land belonging to British Rail.

(5) Waste produced in the course of dredging operations for land drainage or the maintenance of a watercourse which is deposited on the banks of a watercourse.

(6) Waste produced in the maintenance of a park or a recreation ground which is deposited within its boundaries by or with the consent of the occupier.

(7) Waste which is deposited to assess its effect on the environment or which is disposed of to test the efficiency of plant or equipment designed to deal with it.

(8) Waste which is deposited on land for a period not exceeding one month by or with the consent of the occupier, except where waste is temporarily deposited on a site specifically designed for that purpose prior to its ultimate disposal elsewhere.

(9) Waste which is placed in a receptacle with a view to its ultimate disposal elsewhere, provided the deposit is made by or with the consent of the owner of the receptacle.

(10) Waste which is disposed of on the site where it is produced by means of static plant with a disposal capacity not exceeding 200 kg per hour.

(11) Waste which is disposed of as an integral part of the operation which produces it.

(12) Waste deposited by means of pipes (i) on the foreshore, ie, between high and low water marks, and (ii) on any land above high water mark which is covered by the sea from time to time.

It should be noted that s3 does not apply to the deposit of waste on land occupied by a disposal authority for that purpose, or to the use of plant or equipment on such land (see p 73).

Unlicensed deposit of waste

Although criminal sanctions can follow the unlicensed deposit of waste they will not alleviate the problems caused. To achieve this, collection and disposal authorities are given powers to take remedial measures.

If controlled waste is deposited on land in the area of a disposal or a collection authority in contravention of s3(1), the authority may serve a notice on the occupier of the land in question. This can require him either to remove the waste within a specified period of not less than twenty-one days from the receipt of the notice or to take specified steps to eliminate or reduce the consequences of the deposit, or both, within a similar period. The occupier can appeal against the notice to a magistrate's court within the twenty-one day period.

If the court is satisfied that the appellant neither deposited the waste nor knowingly permitted the deposit, or if it is satisfied that the service of the notice was not authorised, eg, no offence under s3 had been committed, or that there was a material defect in the notice, then it must quash the notice.

In any other case the court must modify the notice or dismiss the appeal. The effect of the notice is suspended pending the appeal, and where the court modifies the notice or dismisses the appeal, it may extend the period specified in the notice.

Failure to comply with the terms of a notice is an offence carrying a maximum fine of £400 on summary conviction and £50 for each day on which the offence continues after conviction and before the authority takes action to remedy the situation. Furthermore, the authority may itself take such steps as were specified in the notice and recover from the person in default any expenses reasonably incurred in so doing.

Where there has been a contravention of s3(1), the authority itself may take steps to remove the waste or deal with the effects of the deposit in the following circumstances:

(a) To prevent or remove pollution of water or a danger to public health.
(b) Where there is no occupier of the land in question.
(c) Where the occupier of the land neither made nor knowingly permitted the deposit of waste.

Under this power the authority can recover the costs of removing and disposing of the waste or dealing with the effects of its deposit under (a) from the occupier of the land, unless he proves that he neither made nor caused nor knowingly permitted the deposit, and in any case from the person who made or caused or knowingly permitted the deposit. However, the authority cannot recover such part of the costs as the occupier or other person shows was incurred unnecessarily. **s16**

Disposal Licences

The introduction of a system of licensing is central to the new controls for the disposal of waste. A licence is required if controlled waste is to be deposited on land or if plant or equipment is to be used to deal with such waste.

Applications

An application for a disposal licence must be made to the disposal authority in whose area the land concerned is situated. A licence for land, plant or equipment for which planning permission is necessary must not be issued unless such a permission is in force (see p 178). Regulations may be made to enable an application for a disposal licence to be considered while an application for planning permission is pending, and for any proceedings connected with either application to be conducted with any proceedings concerned with the other.

There is no specific form for an application but, under the Control of Pollution (Licensing of Waste Disposal) Regulations 1976, (SI 1976 No 732, para 5), it must be in writing and contain the following information:

(a) The full name and address of the applicant.

(b) A map showing the location of the land, plant or equipment.

(c) A plan of the layout.

(d) The form of the deposit or disposal for which the licence is sought.

(e) The types and estimated quantities of controlled waste which it is proposed to deposit or dispose of.

(f) Details of any planning permission under the Town and Country Planning Act 1971 which has been granted in respect of the use which is the subject of the application.

Where a disposal authority receives an application for a disposal licence and planning permission is already in force, it must not reject the application unless satisfied that this is necessary to prevent the pollution of water or danger to public health. **s5(3)**

Where a disposal authority proposes to issue a licence, it must first refer the proposal to any water authority and collection authority whose area includes any land involved in the application. It must also refer it to any body prescribed for that purpose. Under the Control of Pollution (Licensing of Waste Disposal) Regulations 1976 (SI 1976 No 732, para 6), these are the Health and Safety Executive and, where the application relates to the deposit of waste underground, the Institute of Geological Science.

The disposal authority must consider any representations made by these other bodies within the period of twenty-one days from the date on which they received the proposals, or such longer period as may be agreed, and in particular, those representations concerning the conditions which should be specified in the licence.

If the water authority requests the disposal authority not to issue the licence, or disagrees with the proposed conditions, either body may refer the application to the Secretary of State. The licence must not then be issued except in accordance with his decision. In effect, this gives a water authority a power of veto over the issue of a disposal licence, subject to a contrary decision by the Secretary of State. **s5(4)**

Finally, if within the period of two months beginning with the date on which the authority receives the application, or such longer period as may be agreed, the authority neither issues the licence nor gives notice that it has rejected the application, then the application will be deemed to have been refused. **s6(5)**

An applicant for a disposal licence who, in his application, knowingly or recklessly makes a statement which is false in a material particular will be guilty of an offence. The maximum penalties are, on summary conviction, a fine of £400, and on conviction on indictment, an unlimited fine, or two years' imprisonment, or both. **s5(2)**

Conditions

The Secretary of State may make regulations specifying the conditions which are or are not to be included in the licence. Subject to these limitations, the conditions which can be imposed are those which the disposal authority thinks appropriate. However, the Act does set out a list of matters which will most commonly be the subject of conditions. These are:

(a) The duration of the licence.

(b) The supervision by the licence-holder of the activities to which the licence relates.

(c) The kinds and quantities of controlled waste which may be dealt with in pursuance of the licence, or so dealt with during a specified period, the methods of dealing with the waste, and the recording of information.

(d) The precautions to be taken on any land to which the licence relates.

(e) The steps to be taken to ensure compliance with the conditions of any relevant planning permission.

(f) The hours during which the waste may be dealt with.

(g) The works to be carried out in connection with the land, plant or equipment to which the licence relates either before the activities authorised in the licence are commenced or while they are continuing.

The conditions imposed may require the licence holder to carry out works or to do some other thing which he is not entitled as of right to do. This means for example that as a condition of the licence he might be required to carry out work on land not owned or occupied by him. This condition does not constitute an order to the owner of that land to allow the licence holder access to carry out the work. **s6(2)**

A failure to observe the conditions of the disposal licence makes the deposit of waste or the use of plant or equipment unlawful and the person responsible is liable to be proceeded against. The Secretary of State may make regulations providing that certain conditions are to be ignored for this purpose, and that non-observance of them does not make an offender liable to the penalties imposed for a breach of s3. A breach of such conditions without reasonable excuse will be an offence subject to a maximum fine on summary conviction of £400, much smaller than penalties for a breach of s3. It appears that conditions relating to minor matters such as administrative requirements can be made subject to this lesser penalty. Proceedings for a breach of such a condition can only be brought by or with the consent of the Director of Public Prosecutions, or by the disposal authority which issued the licence. **s6(3)**

Registers of licences

Each disposal authority must keep a register of all current licences issued by it. This register must be kept open for public inspection at all reasonable times free of charge, and the public must be able, on the payment of a reasonable sum, to obtain copies of entries. Particulars of any resolution passed by the disposal authority are also to be included (see p 73). **s6(4)**

The register must contain the following information in respect of each licence, under the Control of Pollution (Licensing of Waste Disposal) Regulations 1976, (SI 1976 No 732, para 8).

(a) The date the licence was granted.
(b) The full name and address of the licence holder.
(c) The full name and address of the local representative, if any, of the licence holder.
(d) The location of the site to which the licence relates.
(e) The form of deposit or disposal to which the licence relates.
(f) The types of waste of which the deposit or disposal is authorised, and any limitation as to quantity.
(g) Any condition attached to the issue or variation of a licence.

Variation and revocation of licences

Subject to any regulations which specify conditions which are or are not to be included in a disposal licence, a disposal authority has certain powers and duties relating to the variation and revocation of licences.

A disposal authority may serve a notice on a licence holder modifying the specified conditions in the licence to such an extent as it considers desirable, provided that the modification is not likely to cause the licence holder unreasonable expenditure.

Alternatively, the licence holder may apply to the authority requesting it to modify the conditions. If it decides to do so, the authority may then serve a notice on him modifying them as requested. A licence holder who knowingly or recklessly makes a statement in such an application which is false in a material particular commits an offence carrying a maximum penalty on summary conviction of a fine of £400, or on conviction on indictment, an unlimited fine, or two years' imprisonment, or both.

As mentioned previously, regulations may specify those conditions which must or must not be contained in a licence. Where a modification to a licence is necessary to comply with these regulations, the authority must serve a notice making the necessary modifications. An authority must also modify the conditions if it is of the opinion that this is necessary to ensure that the activities covered by the licence do not cause pollution of water, become a danger to public health, or become seriously detrimental to the amenities of the locality affected by the activities.

Except where the modification is necessary to ensure that the licence complies with regulations, the authority must follow the same procedure with regard to consultation as for applications for disposal licences, but:

(1) Reference to the other authorities and bodies may be postponed if necessary because of an emergency, but the reference must be made as soon as possible after the emergency has been dealt with.

(2) The authority may dispense altogether with the reference to the other bodies and authorities if it is of the opinion that the variation will not affect them.

An authority must revoke a licence if it is of the opinion that the activities covered by the licence should not be permitted to continue because of the likelihood of their causing water pollution or danger to public health, or being seriously detrimental to local amenities, and that the risk cannot be removed by a modification of the conditions. In such circumstances the authority has no discretion and must revoke the licence. For revocation after a breach of conditions, see below.

Any notice of modification or revocation must specify the date on which it is to come into effect. **s7**

Transfer and relinquishment

If a licence holder wishes to transfer the licence to another person, he must give notice of the intended transfer to the issuing authority specifying the name and address of the intended transferee, and the date on which it is to take effect.

If during the period of eight weeks beginning with the date on which the authority receives the notice of the intended transfer it gives the transferee notice that it declines to accept him, the licence ceases to have effect at the expiry of ten weeks from the date when the authority received the notice of intended transfer and not from the date of refusal.

Where, by law, the right of the licence holder to occupy the land to which the licence relates is transferred to some other person, then that other person will be deemed to be the holder of the

70

licence for the period of ten weeks from the date of transfer. For instance, if a licence holder is made bankrupt, or dies, and his right to occupy the land passes to his trustee in bankruptcy, or his executor, this gives that person ten weeks in which to sort matters out.

The holder of a licence may relinquish it by delivering it to the issuing authority and giving notice to them that he no longer requires it. **s8**

Supervision and enforcement

While a licence is in force, it is the duty of the issuing authority to take such steps as are necessary to ensure that:

(a) The activities to which the licence relates do not cause the pollution of water or constitute a danger to public health, or become seriously detrimental to local amenities.

(b) Any conditions specified in the licence are complied with.

For these purposes, any officer of the disposal authority who is authorised in writing may, if it appears to him necessary because of an emergency, carry out works on the land, plant or machinery to which the licence relates.

Where the authority incurs expense as a result of this, it can recover the costs from the licence holder, or from the last licence holder if the licence has been revoked or surrendered.

However, costs will not be recoverable if the licence holder or the last licence holder, as the case may be, establishes that there was no emergency, or that the expenditure or some part of it was unnecessary. In the latter case, costs will only be recoverable in respect of the expenses which were necessarily incurred.

Where it appears to an authority that the conditions of a licence are not being complied with it may, without prejudice to any criminal proceedings it might institute, serve a notice on the licence holder requiring him to comply with the conditions within a specified period of time. If, at the end of that period, he has not complied, the authority may serve a further notice revoking the licence at a time specified in the notice, again without prejudice to any possible criminal proceedings. **s9**

Appeals to the Secretary of State

There is provision for appeal to the Secretary of State against a disposal authority's decision in the following circumstances:

(a) Where an application for a disposal licence or any application for a modification of a licence has been rejected.
(b) Where a licence has been issued subject to conditions.
(c) Where the conditions in a licence are modified.
(d) Where a disposal licence is revoked.

Details of the procedure to be followed on appeal are contained in the Control of Pollution (Licensing of Waste Disposal) Regulations 1976 (SI 1976 No 732, para 7), as substituted by the Control of Pollution (Licensing of Waste Disposal) (Amendment) Regulations 1977 (SI 1977 No 1185).

Notice of the appeal must be given in writing within six months of the date of the decision, or such longer period as the Secretary of State may allow. If the subject of the appeal is a deemed rejection under s6(5) (that is, if no decision is given within two months or such longer period as may be agreed, an application will be deemed to be refused), the six months' period runs from the date of the deemed refusal. If he thinks fit, the Secretary of State may require the appellant to furnish, within a specified period, two copies of a statement of his reasons for the appeal, and two copies of any or all of the following:

(1) The application, if any, for the licence or modification.
(2) Any relevant plans, drawings, particulars and documents submitted to the disposal authority in support of the application.
(3) Any relevant record, consent, determination, notice or other notification made or issued by the disposal authority.
(4) Any relevant planning permission.
(5) All other relevant correspondence with other authorities.

The Secretary of State must then send to the disposal authority a copy of the notice of appeal and all other documents submitted by the appellant. He may require the appellant or the disposal authority to submit a further statement concerning any matter to which the appeal relates and if, after considering the grounds of appeal and such further statements, he considers he is sufficiently informed, he may decide the appeal without further investigation.

In any other case he must, if either party so desires, give each of them an opportunity to appear before and be heard by a person appointed for that purpose, unless he decides that a local inquiry should be held.

Where the grounds of appeal are under (c) or (d) above, that is, the modification or revocation of a licence, the general rule is that the decision of the disposal authority is of no effect until the appeal is dismissed or withdrawn. It then takes effect on the date of the dismissal or withdrawal.

There will be no suspension of the authority's decision pending an appeal if the notice of modification or revocation contains a statement that, in the authority's opinion, the effect of the notice should not be suspended in the event of an appeal because of the need to prevent water pollution, or because of danger to public health. In these circumstances the licence holder can apply to the Secretary of State. If the Secretary of State decides that the authority acted unreasonably in including such a statement, if the appeal is still pending, then the decision will be suspended from the day on which that decision was made. If such a decision is made, the licence holder will be entitled to obtain compensation from the authority for any loss he has suffered as a result. Any dispute as to the licence holder's entitlement to compensation, or as to the amount, is to be settled by arbitration. **s10**

The Position of Disposal Authorities

Where a disposal authority itself wishes to dispose of or to deposit waste, a different procedure is required.

Nothing in s3 which bans the deposit of waste or use of plant or equipment without a licence is to apply to waste deposited on land belonging to a disposal authority or to the use of plant or equipment on such land for the treatment of waste, provided that the deposit or use is made either by the disposal authority itself or with the authority's consent, and any conditions imposed by the authority are observed.

However, the use of such land is not free from controls. The authority must ensure that such land is used in accordance with conditions which are calculated to prevent the use of the land causing water pollution, or becoming a danger to public health, or becoming seriously detrimental to the amenities of the locality in which it is situated. These conditions must be specified in a resolution of the authority passed in accordance with the following procedure.

Where the authority proposes to use land for the purpose of the deposit or disposal of waste, it must prepare a statement of conditions which it proposes to include in the resolution, and specifically included or excluded must be any condition which regulations have prescribed must be included in or excluded from a disposal licence.

The proposals must then be referred to any collection authority or water authority whose area includes any of the land specified

73

in the proposal, and to any other specified body—currently the Health and Safety Executive and, where the waste is to be deposited underground, the Institute of Geological Sciences. Any representations made by these bodies within twenty-one days from the date of the receipt of the proposals or such longer period as may be agreed must be considered with particular reference to any conditions which any of the above consider should be included.

The authority must then pass a resolution specifying the conditions which will regulate the use of the land.

Just as a water authority has an effective power of veto over the issue of disposal licences subject to review by the Secretary of State, so it has similar powers in respect of resolutions.

If a water authority requests the disposal authority not to proceed with the resolution or disagrees with the proposed conditions, either the water authority or the disposal authority may refer the matter to the Secretary of State, and the resolution must not then be passed except in accordance with his direction.

A resolution may be varied or rescinded, and must be varied if necessary to include or exclude conditions specified in regulations. Where an authority proposes to alter a resolution, it must follow a similar procedure in that reference must be made to those bodies mentioned above, except where:

(a) The variation is necessary to include or exclude conditions specified in regulations.
(b) The latter resolution merely rescinds the earlier one.
(c) The disposal authority is of the opinion that the variation will not affect the other body.
(d) The variation is required because of an emergency, when the authority may postpone reference to the other body insofar as it considers it appropriate, provided that after the emergency has been dealt with the reference is made as soon as possible.

When it becomes apparent to an authority that the continuation of the activities to which the resolution relates would cause water pollution or be a danger to public health, or be so detrimental to local amenities that they should not be allowed to continue, and that the situation cannot be remedied by an alteration in the conditions, it must rescind the resolution.

Where the water authority in whose area the land to which the resolution relates is situated is of the opinion that the activities are causing or are likely to cause water pollution, it may, without prejudice to any other provision or the possibility of criminal proceedings under Part II of the Act, request the Secretary of State to direct the disposal authority to discontinue its activities.

Particulars of any resolution which is in force must be included in the register of licences which a disposal authority must keep. **s11**

The Refuse Disposal (Amenity) Act 1978

This Act came into force, apart from three minor provisions, on 23 April 1978. Since it deals with local authorities' responsibilities concerning refuse disposal it can conveniently be considered here. The Act consolidates various provisions relating to abandoned vehicles and other refuse—in particular the relevant provisions of the Civic Amenities Act 1967. It should be noted that the following powers and duties are additional to those contained in other legislation such as the Control of Pollution Act 1974 dealing with the problems of waste disposal.

Provision of Facilities

County Councils and the Greater London Council in England and district councils in Wales have a duty to provide places for the deposit of refuse (defined as any matter, whether organic or inorganic) other than refuse disposed of in the course of a business. Although the obligation extends only to non-commercial refuse, an authority may permit on such terms as it thinks fit the deposit at such places of refuse disposed of in the course of business. An authority may provide plant and apparatus for the treatment and disposal of refuse, and may sell or otherwise dispose of it. Instead of providing places for the deposit of refuse itself, the authority may enter into an agreement with some other person whereby that other person provides such facilities.

If the Secretary of State is satisfied, after holding a local inquiry, that an authority has failed to carry out this duty, he may by order require the authority to take specified steps to carry it out. **s1**

Unauthorised Dumping

It is an offence, without lawful authority, to abandon on any land in the open air, or on any land forming part of a highway:

(a) Any motor vehicle.
(b) Anything which has formed part of a motor vehicle and which has been removed from the vehicle in the course of dismantling it on the land.

75

(c) Anything other than a motor vehicle being a thing brought to the land for the purpose of abandoning it there.

The maximum penalties which can be imposed for these offences are, on summary conviction only, a fine of £100 for a first offence, and for a second or subsequent offence, a fine of £200, or three months imprisonment, or both.

If a person leaves anything on land in such circumstances or for such a period that he may reasonably be assumed to have abandoned it, or to have brought it to the land for the purpose of abandoning it, he will be presumed to have abandoned it, or to have brought it to the land for the purpose of abandoning it, unless he can prove otherwise. **s2**

Removal of Abandoned Vehicles and Other Refuse

For the following provisions, except where the contrary is indicated, a local authority is defined as a district council, including a London borough council and the Common Council of the City of London.

Abandoned vehicles

Where it appears to a local authority that a motor vehicle in its area has been abandoned on land in the open air or on land forming part of a highway, it has a duty to remove the vehicle. However, if the land is occupied by any person the authority must give him notice of its intention to remove the vehicle, and if he objects in the prescribed manner the authority will not be permitted to remove the vehicle. Any vehicle removed by a London borough council or the Common Council must be delivered to the Greater London Council, and any vehicle removed by an English district council must be delivered to the relevant county council. Where a local authority proposes to remove a vehicle which is in such a condition that it ought to be destroyed, a notice of its intended removal for destruction must be fixed to the vehicle for a prescribed period before removal. A local authority, a county council or the Greater London Council which has custody of a motor vehicle removed under this section must take reasonable steps for its safe keeping, except where the vehicle has been removed after a notice of intended destruction has been fixed to it. **s3**

A county council or the Greater London Council in England or a district council in Wales may take steps to dispose of a vehicle in the following circumstances. If a notice of intended destruction has been fixed to the vehicle it may be disposed of at any time after its removal if no current licence was displayed on the vehicle at the time of removal, or, if there was a current licence at that time, at any time after the expiry of the licence. In any other case, if prescribed steps have been taken to trace the owner, and either he has not been found or he has failed to comply with a notice requiring him to remove the vehicle from the authority's custody, the authority may dispose of the vehicle after the expiry of any licence in force in respect of the vehicle.

The owner of a vehicle in the custody of an authority may reclaim it on payment of such sums in respect of its removal and storage as may be prescribed. If, before the expiry of one year from the date when a vehicle is sold by an authority, a person satisfies the authority that at that time he was its owner, the authority must pay to him the difference, if any, between the sale price and the total expenses incurred in respect of removal, storage and disposal. **s4**

Where a vehicle is removed, an authority may recover from the person responsible prescribed charges in respect of its removal, storage and disposal. In addition, where a person is convicted of an offence of abandoning a vehicle, the court may, in addition to imposing any penalty, order him to pay to the authority such sum as the court thinks the authority is entitled to recover from him. **s5**

Other refuse

Where anything other than a vehicle is abandoned on land in the open air or on any land forming part of a highway, a local authority may, but need not, remove it. However, if the thing is situated on land which is occupied by any person, a local authority may not exercise its powers unless it has given notice in the prescribed manner and that person has made no objection. A local authority may recover the costs of removing the thing from the person who deposited it, or from a person convicted of an offence. On conviction for an offence, the court may, in addition to any penalty it may impose, order the person convicted to pay to the authority such sums as the authority is entitled to recover in respect of the costs of removing and disposing of the thing. **s6**

Enforcement

Any person authorised in writing by the Secretary of State or a local authority may enter on any land to ascertain whether any of the above functions should be exercised, or to exercise them.

The powers conferred by s281 (1)-(5) of the Town and Country Planning Act 1971 (provisions supplementary to a power of entry) and ss282-4 (provisions relating to local inquiries, the serving of notices, and the furnishing of information) are available for the enforcement of this Act. **s8**

B. COLLECTION PROVISIONS OF THE CONTROL OF POLLUTION ACT 1974

The 1974 Act introduces a new system for the collection of waste by public authorities. This replaces ss72-74 of the Public Health Act 1936.

Responsibility

The prime responsibility for ensuring that there are adequate arrangements for the disposal of waste is placed on disposal authorities, but the position concerning collection prior to disposal is different.

It is the duty of each collection authority to arrange for the collection of all household waste in its area, unless it is in a place which, in the authority's opinion, is so isolated or inaccessible that the cost of collecting it would be unreasonably high and the authority is satisfied that adequate arrangements for its disposal have, or can be, made by the person in control of the waste.

There can be no charge for the collection of household waste except in prescribed cases. Where these charges can be levied, the obligation on the authority to collect the waste does not arise until the person in control of it requests it to do so. In this case the authority may, but need not, recover a reasonable charge from the person who requested the collection.

A collection authority is also under a duty to collect commercial waste from premises in its area if requested to do so by the occupier of the premises, but not otherwise.

An English disposal authority or a collection authority may, if requested by the occupier of premises in its area, arrange for the collection of industrial waste, but no authority is under an obligation to do so. Furthermore, before an English collection authority is entitled to collect industrial waste, it must obtain the consent of the disposal authority which has to receive and deal with the waste delivered to it.

A person who requests the collection of waste other than household waste has to pay a reasonable charge for its collection and disposal to the collection authority. This charge must be collected by the authority unless in the case of commercial waste it considers it appropriate to waive it. An authority has no power to waive charges for the collection and disposal of industrial waste.

A collection authority must make arrangements for the emptying of privies serving private dwellings in its area, and can make no charge. If requested, it must also empty cesspools serving private dwellings in its area, but may, if it considers it appropriate, impose a reasonable charge. A collection authority may also, if requested, empty other cesspools and privies in its area at a reasonable charge.

A collection authority may contribute towards the cost incurred by another person in providing or maintaining plant or equipment to deal with household waste before it is collected. Similarly, a collection authority or an English disposal authority may contribute to the cost of plant or equipment to deal with commercial or industrial waste before it is collected.

Unless any other provision is made, any waste collected by an authority belongs to that authority and may be dealt with accordingly. **s12**

Receptacles

These powers are to be exercised subject to any relevant regulations which might be made concerning the following:

(a) The size, construction and maintenance of receptacles.
(b) The placing of receptacles on premises to facilitate their emptying, and access to them for that purpose.
(c) The placing of receptacles on highways for the purpose of facilitating their emptying, with the consent of the highways authority, and the question of liability caused by receptacles so placed.
(d) The substances which may and may not be placed in receptacles and the precautions to be taken when particular substances are placed in them.
(e) The steps to be taken by occupiers of premises to facilitate the collection of waste from receptacles.
(f) The giving of directions concerning the above by collection authorities, and compliance with those directions.
(g) The imposition of a maximum fine of £100 on summary conviction for non-compliance with the regulations or directions given in pursuance of regulations.

79

Household Waste

Where a collection authority is under a duty to arrange for the collection of household waste, it may serve a notice on the occupier of any premises within its area requiring him to place the waste in receptacles of a specified kind. Failure to comply is an offence carrying a maximum fine on summary conviction of £100.

Such a notice may provide for the receptacles to be provided by the authority free of charge or, if the recipient agrees, to be provided by the authority on payment of a single or periodical payments. If the recipient of the notice does not enter into such an agreement within a period specified in the notice or the notice contains no provisions for such an agreement, he must supply the receptacle himself.

Where the recipient is obliged to supply receptacles, he may, within twenty-one days from the end of the period for entering into an agreement or from the date of the receipt of the notice if there is no such period, appeal against the notice to a magistrate's court. The grounds of appeal are that the kind or number of receptacles specified is unreasonable, or that the receptacles already provided are adequate.

If there is such an appeal, the notice will be suspended pending the determination of the appeal. The court may quash or modify the notice, or dismiss the appeal.

Where there is an appeal, no question as to whether the kind or number of receptacles specified in the notice is unreasonable can be entertained in any proceedings for an offence concerning the notice.

Commercial and Industrial Waste

An English disposal authority or a collection authority may, if requested, supply receptacles for the storage of commercial and industrial waste which it has been asked to collect. A reasonable charge must be imposed for any receptacle provided but this may be waived by the authority in the case of commercial waste only, if it considers it appropriate to do so.

Where a collection authority is of the opinion that there is likely to be stored in its area commercial or industrial waste which, if not kept in receptacles, will be likely to cause a nuisance or be detrimental to the amenities of the locality, it can serve a notice on the occupier of the premises requiring him to provide specified receptacles for the storage of the waste. Failure to comply with the notice is an offence with a maximum penalty on summary conviction of £100.

The recipient of the notice can appeal against it to a magistrate's court within twenty-one days from the date of receipt of the notice. The grounds of the appeal are that the kind and number of receptacles specified is unreasonable, or that the waste is not likely to cause a nuisance or be detrimental to the amenities of the locality. The court may quash or modify the notice, or dismiss the appeal.

As with household waste, the effect of the notice will be suspended until the appeal is determined. Where there is an appeal, the question of the reasonableness of the kind or number of receptacles cannot be raised in any proceedings for an offence concerning the notice. **s13**

Disposal

Once the waste has been collected it must be disposed of. Basically, a collection authority must deliver to the relevant disposal authority at such places as that authority may direct, all waste collected except waste paper which it decides to retain. This then becomes the disposal authority's property, and may be dealt with accordingly.

This arrangement can be varied by express agreement between the disposal and collection authorities concerned. They may agree, subject to conditions as to payment and other specified matters, that waste to which the agreement relates shall not be delivered to the disposal authority but shall be retained by the collection authority with a view to recycling or reclamation. Without prejudice to any other powers, a collection authority may provide plant and equipment for the purpose of baling and sorting waste paper, or for sorting or processing other waste which it retains.

A disposal authority may provide sites, plant and equipment either within or outside its own area for processing or otherwise disposing of waste which has either been delivered to it or collected by it. It can also provide places, either within or outside its area, for the deposit of waste prior to its transportation to another site for final disposal.

Collection or disposal authorities may permit other persons to use these facilities. They may also provide for other people facilities similar to those which can be established for their own use. However, except in the case of household waste when no charge can be made, the authority must make a reasonable charge for the use of these facilities, unless it considers it appropriate not to do so.

Anything delivered to an authority by a person making use of the facilities provided will belong to the authority and can be dealt with accordingly.

When a collection authority delivers commercial or industrial waste to a disposal authority under these provisions, the disposal authority can recover from the collection authority such a sum as represents the reasonable cost of the disposal. The collection authority's charge for the collection of waste includes an element for its disposal. Where the disposal authority requires the delivery of waste to a place which is an unreasonable distance from the collection authority's area, the collection authority is entitled to a reasonable contribution towards the cost of transport. A dispute as to the reasonableness of either of these matters is to be settled by arbitration.

The position regarding payments can be altered by agreement between the authorities concerned. They may agree on payments by one to the other concerning waste collected by the collection authority. In particular, mention is made in the Act of payment to the collection authority in respect of waste which is retained with a view to recycling or reclamation.

The definition of waste for the above purpose does not include matter removed from privies or cesspools for which separate provision is made. In this case the collection authority must deliver the matter removed in accordance with directions given by the relevant water authority.

The directions must specify the place to which it is to be delivered, either to the water authority or to some other person, and this must be a reasonable distance from the collection authority's area. From time to time the collection authority must give a statement to the water authority of the amount of such matter which it expects to deliver to or as directed by the water authority, during such periods as may be specified. Any dispute as to whether a place is a reasonable distance is to be determined by arbitration. Any matter so delivered becomes the property of the water authority and it is entitled to charge for receiving it. **s14**

C. MISCELLANEOUS PROVISIONS

Dangerous Waste

Dangerous waste comes under the system of controls discussed above. One provision, the higher penalties for the unlicensed deposit of waste which causes an environmental hazard, has been dealt with above.

In some circumstances the general scheme of the Act will not provide sufficiently stringent measures to deal with particularly hazardous waste. Accordingly, the Act makes provisions for a category of 'special waste'. This is defined as waste which is so dangerous or difficult to dispose of that special provision is required to regulate its disposal by disposal authorities or other persons.

Details such as precautions to be taken and the sorts of waste which will come within the definition are left to be dealt with in regulations, but the Act does lay down in general terms the scheme of controls.

Where the Secretary of State is satisfied that waste is of such a character as to comply with the definition of special waste and to require special provisions for its disposal, he is under a duty to make regulations for that purpose. Although there is no limit set on what can be covered in the regulations, the Act does contain a list of what are likely to be the more common matters. These are:

(a) The giving of directions by disposal authorities with respect to matters concerning the disposal of special waste.

(b) To secure that special waste is not, while awaiting disposal in accordance with regulations, kept at any one place in quantities greater or in circumstances which differ from those laid down in regulations.

(c) To require the occupier of premises on which special waste is situated to give notice of the fact and other prescribed information to a prescribed authority.

(d) To secure that records are kept by persons who produce special waste, dispose of it or transfer it to another person for disposal, to provide for the inspection of such records and for the furnishing to prescribed authorities of copies of the records or information derived from them.

(e) To provide that contravention of the regulations will be a criminal offence and prescribe the maximum penalties which shall not in any case exceed a fine of £400 on summary conviction, or, on conviction on indictment, two years' imprisonment, or an unlimited fine, or both.

(f) To provide that special waste of particular kinds shall be disposed of only by disposal authorities or, if the Secretary of State considers that there is such a risk or damage to persons, animals or vegetation that it should be disposed of only by him, by the Secretary of State.

(g) For the supervision by disposal authorities of activities authorised by regulations which can be achieved either by a modification to the general provisions of s9 or otherwise.

(h) For the recovery of expenses and other charges by the Secretary of State or disposal authorities for disposal in pursuance of regulations.

(i) For appeals to the Secretary of State from decisions of disposal authorities.

(j) Where there is a disposal licence or an authority's resolution in force for a particular place, to provide for the giving of directions requiring the licence holder or authority to accept and dispose of specified special waste at that place and upon such terms including payment as may be specified in the direction.

(k) As to the consents obtained and the other steps to be taken before such a direction can be given and as to appeals to the Secretary of State against such a direction.

(l) To provide that failure to comply with such a direction shall be an offence punishable on summary conviction with a fine not exceeding £400 or such lesser sum as may be specified, and to exempt a person from liability under any specified enactment for any act or omission necessarily done in order to comply with the direction. **s17**

It should also be noted that under s101 the United Kingdom Atomic Energy Authority is given powers to engage in the UK and elsewhere in the treatment and disposal of such waste as the Secretary of State may specify in a notice. This power is not limited to waste which is radioactive. Presumably it will be used where waste is so difficult and dangerous to dispose of that it should be subject to precautions as stringent as those required when dealing with radioactive materials.

Waste other than Controlled Waste

The definition of controlled waste specifically excludes agricultural waste, and waste from mines and quarries. However, the Secretary of State, after consultation with such bodies as he thinks fit, may make regulations to extend to such waste all or any part of ss1–11, and ss14–17, ie, all the above provisions except those relating to the collection of waste, and receptacles. Such regulations may extend the controls only in specified areas, and make such modifications to the above sections as are necessary. The regulations can also modify any other enactment to such an extent as the Secretary of State considers appropriate.

Irrespective of whether the controls have been extended by regulations, certain provisions relating to collection and receptacles in the Act are applicable to waste other than controlled waste. An English disposal authority and a collection authority may, if requested by an owner or occupier of premises, arrange for the collection of waste other than controlled waste. The authority which arranges the collection must impose and collect a reasonable charge for doing so, and an English collection authority is only entitled to exercise this power if it has obtained the consent of the relevant disposal authority.

An English disposal authority or a collection authority may also, at the request of any person, supply him with receptacles for waste other than controlled waste which he has asked to be collected, and must make a reasonable charge for doing so.

A disposal authority has powers to collect information about, and to make arrangements for the disposal of waste other than controlled waste which is, or is likely to be, situated in its area. However, if it does so, it is not entitled to exercise the powers contained in ss91–94 (see p 156).

Although certain types of waste are not included in the definition of controlled waste, this does not mean that waste not coming within the definition can be deposited with impunity. Irrespective of whether the general controls have been extended by regulations, where a person deposits on land waste other than controlled waste or causes or knowingly permits such a deposit he will, in certain circumstances, be guilty of an offence under s18(2).

An offence will be committed where, had the waste been controlled waste, an offence under s3(3) would have been committed, ie, where the waste is poisonous, noxious or polluting, and its presence on the land is likely to give rise to an environmental hazard, and it is deposited in such circumstances as to indicate that it has been abandoned.

The penalties are the same as for a contravention of s3(3). In addition to the defences under s3, it will also be a defence to show that the deposit was made in pursuance of and in accordance with the terms of a consent, licence, approval, or authority granted under any enactment, but a planning permission of itself is not sufficient.
ss18, 19

Civil Liability for the Deposit of Waste

Generally, the aim of the Act is to compel compliance with the various provisions upon pain of criminal sanctions. However, in certain circumstances, the Act imposes civil liability where an unlicensed deposit causes damage, and the person in default will be liable to compensate anyone who has suffered injury. It should be stressed that civil liability imposed by the Act is independent of any liability under the general law of tort (see Chapter 1).

To incur civil liability there must have been a deposit of poisonous, noxious or polluting waste in circumstances such that an offence under s3(3) or s18(2) has been committed, ie, there can be civil liability for the deposit of both controlled waste and waste other than controlled waste, provided that, in either case, the waste is poisonous, noxious or polluting, its presence is likely to give rise to an environmental hazard, and it is deposited in circumstances which indicate that it has been abandoned. An offence under either of the above sections must have been committed, although a conviction is not a prerequisite.

The person who deposited the waste or who caused or knowingly permitted its deposit is liable to compensate for the damage caused by the deposit, unless the damage was due wholly to the fault of the person who suffered it or was suffered by persons who voluntarily accepted the risk.

Certain of the defences available to someone charged with a criminal offence are equally available as a defence to an action for damages. The defendant will not be liable if:

(a) He took care to ascertain from persons in a position to know that the deposit would not be in contravention of the Act, and neither knew nor had reason to suspect that the information given was false or misleading and that the deposit would be an offence.

(b) He acted on the instructions of his employer and neither knew nor had reason to suspect that the deposit would be in contravention of the Act.

(c) Where the contravention occurred by reason of a failure to observe conditions in a licence, he took all steps reasonably open to ensure compliance.

It should be noted that the remaining defence to a criminal charge, that of acting in an emergency, is not available when civil liability is in issue. **s88**

Recycling and Reclamation

A collection authority has the power to retain waste paper and establish facilities to deal with it, and by agreement with the disposal authority it can retain waste for recycling and reclamation (see under Disposal, p 81). Specific provision is made for recycling and reclamation to be considered when a waste disposal plan is being prepared. In addition, there are other provisions relating to this problem.

A disposal authority may do such things as it thinks fit to enable waste to be used again or to enable substances to be reclaimed from it. These powers can be exercised in respect of its own waste or of waste belonging to another person who asks the authority to deal with it under these provisions. A disposal authority may buy or otherwise acquire waste with a view to its being recycled or to substances being reclaimed from it, and it can use, sell or otherwise dispose of waste it owns, or anything produced from it. **s20**

A disposal authority may use its own waste for the purpose of producing heat and may establish installations for that purpose either in or outside its area. It can use other fuel in combination with the waste and, in an emergency, use fuel other than waste. It can also use, sell or otherwise dispose of the heat produced. As soon as practicable after the end of each year in which it uses an installation to produce heat, it must send the Secretary of State such particulars of the installation and the heat produced as are prescribed.

It may also use waste to produce electricity and can establish, either within or outside its area, generating stations and other installations for this purpose, and use other fuel to assist in the burning of the waste. In an emergency it can use other fuel than waste to produce electricity. The authority may itself use the electricity at the installation where it was produced, and on any premises used in connection with the installation, but it is not allowed to use it elsewhere.

Before being allowed to generate electricity for any other use, the authority must first have consultations with the Central Electricity Generating Board and any other Electricity Board involved, and any arrangements must be approved by the Secretary of State. Where an authority produces electricity for any use otherwise than as allowed under the above provisions, it must sell it to any Electricity Board specified in the arrangements, upon terms set out, and may not sell or otherwise dispose of it to any other person. As a corollary, once the arrangements have been made, any specified

Electricity Board must buy the electricity in accordance with the terms of the arrangement. **s21**

D. ENFORCEMENT

An authority has the enforcement powers contained in the Control of Pollution Act to enforce the relevant provisions of that Act (see p 156).

CHAPTER FOUR

THE CONTROL OF NOISE

The statutory control of noise is of comparatively recent origin. The Noise Abatement Act 1960 was passed in an attempt to tackle the problem by extending the statutory nuisance provisions of the Public Health Act 1936 to cover noise or vibration. This Act has been replaced by Part III of the Control of Pollution Act 1974, all of which came into force on 1 January 1976.

This chapter is concerned with what may be termed neighbourhood noise: this is noise which adversely affects the area surrounding the premises in which it arises. The problems of noise within the workplace and the effect of sound levels on the workforce are regulated by legislation relating to health and safety at work.

The relevant common law principles must be mentioned first (see Chapter I). A person affected by noise may be able to take action in negligence or public or private nuisance, the last being by far the most likely. However, such a remedy is subject to the restrictions inherent in the use of tort, and the annoyance caused must be substantial, and not trivial.

A recent example of a common law action to restrain noise can be seen in the case of Allison v Merton, Sutton and Wandsworth Area Health Authority. The plaintiff was the tenant of a local authority building adjoining the boiler house of a hospital run by the defendants. After the boilers were converted in January 1974, the plaintiff was affected by low-frequency sound. This continued in spite of attempts to reduce the sound level in October. He suffered depression and nervous trouble, and had difficulty in sleeping, but there was no significant injury to his health. In this case the plaintiff was awarded £850 damages, and an injunction to restrain the nuisance was granted, but its effect was suspended for twelve months to enable the defendants to remedy the situation.

Control of Pollution Act 1974

The authorities with the responsibility for enforcing Part III of the Act are local authorities, defined as in England or Wales a district council or borough council, the Common Council of the City of London, the Sub-Treasurer of the Inner Temple, and the Under Treasurer of the Middle Temple.

A local authority must initiate periodical inspections of its area to detect anything which ought to be dealt with under s58, and to decide how to exercise its powers concerning noise abatement zones. An authority's area, except for the provisions relating to noise in streets and noise abatement zones, includes territorial waters adjacent to it, and references to premises and occupier include a vessel and the master of a vessel. Noise for these purposes also includes vibration.

Summary Proceedings to Deal with Noise

1. Proceedings by local authorities

Notices

Where a local authority is satisfied that noise amounting to a nuisance (presumably nuisance here has its common law meaning in that it must be substantial and in some way affect the enjoyment of property rights), exists or is likely to occur or recur in its area, it must serve a notice. (Unlike the Public Health Act 1936 statutory nuisance provisions, a noise nuisance need not exist for a local authority to be able to take action nor, as under the Public Health (Recurring Nuisances) Act 1969, need it have occurred.)

This notice must impose all or some of the following requirements:

(a) Requiring the abatement of the nuisance, or prohibiting or restricting its occurrence or recurrence.
(b) Requiring the execution of such works and the taking of such other steps as may be necessary for the purpose of the notice, or as may be specified in the notice.

A notice must also specify the time limits within which the requirements of the notice must be complied with.

The notice must be served on the person responsible for the nuisance or, if he cannot be found or the nuisance has not yet occurred, on the owner or occupier of the premises from which the noise is or would be emitted.

Failure without reasonable excuse to comply with the notice is an offence, but in proceedings for an alleged non-compliance certain defences are available. These are:

(1) If the noise is produced in the course of a trade or a business, it is a defence to prove that the best practicable means have been used to prevent or counteract the effect of the noise.
(2) In proceedings for a contravention of a notice imposing any of the requirements contained in (a) above, but not (b), that
   (i) The alleged offence was covered by a notice served under s60 (construction sites), a consent given under s61 (construction sites), or a consent given under s65 (consent to a noise level in a noise abatement zone).
   (ii) The alleged offence was committed at a time when the premises were subject to a notice served under s66, that is, a noise reduction notice, and the level of noise was not such as to constitute a contravention of that notice.
   (iii) Although a noise reduction notice had not been served under s66, a noise level fixed under s67 applied to the premises and the level of noise from the premises did not exceed it.

Where the nuisance appears to have been caused wholly or partly by acts or defaults committed or taking place outside its area, the authority may take action as if the cause of the nuisance were situated within its area, except that any appeal will be heard by a magistrate's court having jurisdiction in the place where the act or default is alleged to have taken place.

If the authority is of the opinion that proceedings in a magistrate's court would provide an inadequate remedy, it may take proceedings in the High Court to secure the abatement, prohibition or restriction of the nuisance, although it has not itself suffered any damage. In such proceedings it will be a defence to prove that the noise was authorised by a notice issued under s60 or a consent given under s61.

This section supersedes and replaces s1 of the Noise Abatement Act 1960, except that notices issued under the 1960 Act remain effective. **s58**

A recent case has examined the effect of this section. In Hammersmith Borough Council v Magnum Automated Forecourts, residents complained to the local authority about the noise coming from a twenty-four hour taxi-care centre. The local authority served a notice on the company requiring it to cease operations between 11 pm and 7 am. The company appealed against the notice to a magistrate's court and continued to operate the centre in contravention of the notice. They were not entitled to do this as the general rule, applicable in this case, is that the effect of a notice will not be suspended because an appeal against it is lodged.

Instead of prosecuting for non-compliance with the notice, the local authority took proceedings in the High Court for an injunction, and the magistrates then adjourned the appeal. In the High Court the application was refused, the judge holding that an injunction could not be granted as the statutory proceedings had not been exhausted. The local authority appealed against this decision to the Court of Appeal which held that the authority was entitled to an injunction to stop the activities rather than having to continue with the proceedings in the magistrate's court.

A court can award an injunction to ensure compliance with such a notice, although if it is found eventually that there was no nuisance and that the notice was not justified, the local authority will be liable to pay compensation.

Appeals against notices

A person on whom a notice is served has a right to appeal to a magistrate's court within the period of twenty-one days from the date of service, and the notice must contain a statement of his right of appeal.

The details relating to appeals are contained in the Control of Noise (Appeals) Regulations 1975 (SI 1975 No 2116, para 4). The grounds of appeal may include such of the following as are appropriate:

(a) That the notice is not justified by the terms of s58, eg, that the noise does not amount to a nuisance.
(b) That there has been some informality, defect or error in connection with the notice, but where the error was not material the court must dismiss the appeal.
(c) That the local authority has unreasonably refused to accept compliance with alternative requirements, or that the requirements of the notice are otherwise unreasonable in character or extent or are unnecessary.
(d) That any time limit within which the requirement of the notice must be complied with is not sufficient.

(e) Where the noise is caused in the course of a trade or business, that the best practicable means have been used to prevent it or counteract its effect.

(f) That the requirements imposed by the notice are more onerous than the requirements relating to the same noise of a notice under s60 or s66, a consent given under s61 or s65, or a determination under s67.

(g) That the notice should have been served on some person other than the appellant, being the person responsible for the noise.

(h) That the notice might lawfully have been served on some person other than or in addition to the appellant, being the owner or occupier of the premises from which the noise is or would be emitted, and that it would have been equitable for it to have been so served.

(i) That the notice might lawfully have been served on some person in addition to the appellant, being a person also responsible for the noise, and that it would have been equitable for it to have been so served.

Where the grounds of appeal include (h) or (i) above, the appellant must serve a copy of the notice of appeal on the person referred to, and in the case of an appeal on any of the above grounds, he may serve a copy on any person having an interest on the premises in question.

On hearing the appeal, the court may dismiss it, quash the notice, or vary it in favour of the appellant. Such a varied notice is final and has effect as if made in that form by the local authority. The court has no power to vary the notice so as to impose more onerous terms on the appellant.

The court may make such order as it thinks fit with respect to the person by whom any works are to be carried out, the contribution to be made by any person to the cost of the works, and the proportion in which any expenses which may be recoverable by the local authority are to be borne by the appellant and any other person. In making this order, the court must have regard to the terms of any lease and the nature of the works required in apportioning responsibilities between an owner and an occupier,

Before any requirement is imposed on any person other than the appellant, the court must be satisfied that that other person has received a copy of the notice of appeal.

Default powers of local authorities

Where a notice requiring works to be carried out is served and the person responsible fails to do them, the local authority may carry them out. It may recover the costs unless the person in default can show that all or some of the expenditure was unnecessary. **s69**

2. Proceedings by an occupier of premises

An individual affected by noise may attempt to remedy the situation by requesting a local authority to exercise the powers outlined above. Alternatively, an occupier of premises may take action in a magistrate's court alleging that he is aggrieved by noise amounting to a nuisance. It must be noted that in this case the nuisance must either exist or have occurred. He cannot take action if a nuisance is likely, although a local authority can.

Proceedings under this section are to be brought against the person responsible for the noise or, if he cannot be found, against the owner or occupier of the premises from which it is emitted.

If the court is satisfied that the nuisance exists or that if abated, it is likely to recur, it must make an order for one or both of the following:

(a) Requiring the defendant to abate the nuisance within a specified time and to carry out any necessary works for the purpose.

(b) Prohibiting a recurrence of the nuisance and requiring the defendant to carry out any necessary works for the purpose within a specified time.

If, without a reasonable excuse, he fails to comply, he will be guilty of an offence. In proceedings for a contravention of such an order, it is a defence to show that where the noise was caused in the course of a trade or business, the best practicable means have been used to prevent or counteract its effect. None of the other defences available when a notice issued by a local authority has been contravened are available under this section. **s59**

If a person is convicted of an offence of failing to comply with an order, the court, after giving the local authority an opportunity to be heard, may direct it to do anything which that person was ordered to do under the order. In addition, where a person fails to carry out works specified in the order, the local authority, on its own initiative, may carry out those works. In either case, the local authority may recover the cost of those works from the person in default, except insofar as the expenses are shown to have been unnecessarily incurred. **s59(6), s69**

Control of Noise on Construction Sites

Definition

For the first time local authorities are given extensive powers to control noise on construction sites. These powers can be exercised in respect of the following works:

(a) The erection, construction, alteration, repair or maintenance of buildings, structures or roads.
(b) Breaking up, opening or boring under any road or adjacent land in connection with the construction, inspection, maintenance, or removal of works.
(c) Demolition or dredging work.
(d) Any work of engineering construction whether or not also contained in (a), (b) or (c) above.

Notices

Where it appears to a local authority that any of the above works are being or are about to be carried out, it may serve a notice imposing requirements as to the way in which the works may be carried out. This notice must be served on the person who is carrying out or is about to carry out the works, and on such other person appearing to be responsible for or to have control over the works, as the authority thinks fit. In addition, it may publicise the contents of the notice.

In particular, the notice may:

(a) Specify the plant or machinery which are or are not to be used.
(b) Specify the hours during which the works may be carried out.
(c) Specify the level of noise which may be emitted from the premises in question or at any specified point on those premises, or which may be so emitted during specified hours.
(d) Make provision for changed circumstances.

In addition, the notice may specify a time limit within which the notice is to be complied with, and may require the execution of such works and the taking of such other steps as may be necessary for the purposes of the notice, or as may be specified. The authority may also include such other matters as it thinks fit.

When an authority is using these powers, it must have regard to various matters specified in the Act. These are:

(a) The provision of any code of practice issued under this part of the Act. A code of practice has been approved for these purposes as from 1 January 1976. This is the BSI Code of Practice for noise control on construction and demolition sites (BS 5228: 1975).
(b) The need for ensuring that the best practicable means are used to minimise noise.
(c) Before specifying any particular methods, plant or machinery, considering whether any others would be substantially as effective in minimising the noise and more acceptable to the recipients of the notice.
(d) The need to protect persons in the locality from the effects of the noise.

Contravention of such a notice without reasonable excuse is an offence. **s60**

Appeals against notices

A person served with such a notice has a right of appeal within twenty-one days of the date of service of the notice to a magistrate's court. The notice must contain a statement of this right of appeal.

The details of the appeal procedure are contained in the Control of Noise (Appeals) Regulations 1975 (SI 1975 No 2116, para 5).

The grounds of appeal may include such of the following as are appropriate:

(a) That the notice is not justified in the terms of s.60.
(b) That there has been some informality, defect or error in or in connection with the notice.
(c) That the authority has refused unreasonably to accept compliance with alternative requirements or that the requirements of the notice are unreasonable in character or extent, or are otherwise unnecessary.
(d) That a time limit within which any requirement must be complied with is not reasonably sufficient for the purpose.
(e) That the notice should have been served on some person other than the appellant, being a person who is carrying out the works or is about to do so, or who is responsible for or has control over the works.
(f) That the notice might lawfully have been served on some person in addition to the appellant, being a person who is carrying out works or is about to carry out works or who is responsible for or has control over the works, and that it would have been equitable for it to have been so served.

(g) That the authority has not considered any of the matters which it was obliged to consider before issuing the notice.

Where the appeal is under (e) or (f), the appellant must serve a copy of the notice on the person referred to. In the case of an appeal on any grounds, he may serve a copy on any person having an interest in the premises in question.

Where the appeal is under (b), the court must dismiss the appeal if it is satisfied that the informality, defect or error was not material. In any other case, the court may dismiss the appeal, quash the notice, or vary the notice in such a manner as it thinks fit in favour of the appellant but not against him. A notice which is so varied shall be final and have effect as if originally made in that form by the local authority.

Prior consent for work on construction sites

An alternative procedure to the imposition of conditions by a notice is by prior consent to a noise level. Where a person intends to carry out any works in the above definition, he may apply to the local authority for consent. If approval under the Building Regulations is necessary for the proposed works, the application for consent must be made at the same time as or later than the request for Building Regulations approval.

The application must contain particulars of the works and the methods by which they will be carried out and details of the steps which it is proposed to take to minimise noise. If the authority considers that the application contains sufficient information and that if the works are carried out in accordance with the application, a notice under the preceding power would not be served, it must give consent to the application.

In dealing with applications for consent, the authority must consider, before making a decision, those matters which it must consider in deciding whether to issue a notice—any code of practice, the best practicable means, suitable alternatives, and the protection of persons in the locality.

The authority must give notice of its decision within twenty-eight days and may take such steps to publicise the consent as it thinks fit. This consent must contain a statement that it does not of itself provide a defence in proceedings instituted under s59 by an occupier of premises.

The authority's consent may be given subject to conditions, or limited or qualified to allow for a change in circumstances, or limited as to its duration. Contravention of a condition is an offence.

Where the works are to be carried out by a person other than the applicant, he must take reasonable steps to bring the consent to the notice of that other person. Failure to do so is an offence. **s61**

Appeals

Where the authority refuses its consent, or fails to give a decision within twenty-eight days, or gives consent which is limited or qualified in any way, or is subject to conditions, the applicant may appeal to a magistrate's court within twenty-one days of the end of the twenty-eight day period. A statement of this right of appeal must be contained in any document giving the authority's decision. The details of the procedure are contained in the Control of Noise (Appeals) Regulations, 1975 (SI 1975 No 2116, para 6). There are two sets of provisions, one dealing with appeals where consent has been given but is qualified in some way, and the other where consent has been refused or the authority has failed to give a decision.

Qualified consent   Where the authority has given consent subject to conditions or the consent is qualified or limited in some way, the grounds of appeal may include such of the following as are appropriate:

(a) That any condition, qualification or limitation is not justified in the terms of s.61.
(b) That there has been some informality, defect or error in or in connection with the consent.
(c) That the requirements of any condition, etc, are unreasonable in character or extent, or are unnecessary.
(d) That any time limit within which any requirement of a condition is to be complied with is not reasonably sufficient.

Where the grounds of appeal are under (b), the court must dismiss the appeal if satisfied that the error, defect or informality is not material. In any other case the court may dismiss the appeal, quash any relevant condition, or vary the consent or any condition in favour of the appellant. A condition or consent so varied shall be final and have effect as if made in that form by the local authority.

Refusal or failure to give consent   Where the appeal is concerned with the refusal of an authority to give consent or the failure of the authority to give any decision within the twenty-eight day period, on hearing the appeal the court must give the appellant and the local authority an opportunity to be heard and to make representations concerning the application and any conditions which they consider appropriate.

The court may either adjourn the appeal to enable the appellant to submit a fresh application or it may itself make an order giving consent either unconditionally or subject to such conditions as it thinks fit. If the court gives consent, it must consider all the matters which must be taken into consideration by a local authority and any others which appear relevant. Any such consent is final and shall have effect as if originally made in that form by the local authority.

Noise in Streets

A loudspeaker must not be used in a street for any purpose between the hours of 9 pm and 8 am, and must not be used at any other time for the purpose of advertising an entertainment or business.

There are two exceptions to this general prohibition. It does not apply to loudspeakers operated by the police, fire and ambulance services, water authorities, local authorities, or in an emergency. In addition, a loudspeaker may be used between 12 noon and 7 pm for the purpose of informing the public that a perishable commodity for human consumption is for sale, provided that it is so operated as not to give cause for annoyance. The use of a loudspeaker in contravention of this provision is an offence. **s62**

Noise Abatement Zones

The 1974 Act contains new provisions to enable local authorities to declare all or part of their areas to be noise abatement zones within which they will have increased powers to regulate and control noise and to attempt to reduce the level of noise. It should be noted that the following powers can only be exercised within a noise abatement zone and do not apply in other areas.

Designation

A local authority may designate all or any part of its area a noise abatement zone by a noise abatement order confirmed by the Secretary of State. Such an order must specify the class or classes of premises to which it relates, ie, the sorts of premises which will be subject to the following controls. The order may be varied or

99

revoked by a similar procedure. The detailed procedure is contained in Schedule I to the Act.

After the authority has made the draft order, it must serve on every owner, lessee and occupier, other than tenants for a month or less, of any premises to which the order relates, and publish in the London Gazette, and once at least in each of two successive weeks in a newspaper circulating in the area to which the order relates, a notice containing:

(a) A statement that the order has been made, and an indication of its general effect.
(b) Details of a place in the area of the local authority where a copy of the order and any plan or map referred to may be inspected by any person, free of charge, at all reasonable times during a period of not less than six weeks from the date of the notice.
(c) A statement that within that period any person who will be affected by the order may object to the Secretary of State against the confirmation of the order.

Where no objection is made, or any objection made is withdrawn, the Secretary of State may confirm the order with or without modifications. In any other case the Secretary of State must either cause a local inquiry to be held or afford any person who has made an objection an opportunity to be heard before a person appointed for that purpose. After considering the report of the person who held the inquiry or hearing, the Secretary of State may confirm the order with or without modifications.

He may ignore these requirements if he is of the opinion that compliance is not necessary having regard to the nature of the premises to which the order relates, or the nature of the interests of those who have made objections.

Where an order varies or revokes a previous order, the Secretary of State may disregard any objection which, in his opinion, amounts in substance to an objection made to the previous order.

The order must specify the date on which it is to come into effect. This must be not less than one month from the date of confirmation, except in the case of an order revoking or varying a previous order by excluding from it a specified class of premises, when it can come into effect at any time.

Before the date when the order is due to come into effect, a local authority can postpone it by passing a resolution and publishing a notice of it in the London Gazette and once at least in each of two successive weeks in a local newspaper. This can be postponed yet again, but if the period or periods of the postponement total more than twelve months, the consent of the Secretary of State is necessary.

Register of noise levels

After the noise abatement zone has been designated, the local authority must measure the noise level coming from premises in the zone which are of a class to which the order applies. The places where the measurements are to be taken are to be determined by the local authority.

The methods to be used for measurement are set out in the Control of Noise (Measurement and Registers) Regulations 1976 (SI 1976 No 37). The details are contained in the Schedule to the regulations. It should be noted that these methods are not exhaustive and if the Secretary of State is satisfied that alternative methods would facilitate the measurement of noise levels, he may authorise their use.

All measurements must be recorded in a noise level register which must be available for public inspection at the authority's principal office at all reasonable hours, free of charge, and the public must be able to obtain copies of entries on payment of a reasonable fee.

The contents of the registers are laid down in the above regulations. They must contain:

(a) The address or other sufficient identification of the premises and the specified class to which they belong.
(b) Details of the noise level recorded and particulars of the methods used and details of measurements and calculations, including the location and height of each point where they were taken or for which calculations were made, details of any equipment used, the dates and times when the measurements were taken, and details of the prevailing weather conditions.
(c) Any cancellation or alteration of an entry in the register, and the reasons for it.
(d) The date of each entry, cancellation or alteration.
(e) An index which may be in the form of, or include, a map.

The register may also contain information such as photographs and plans, and may take the form the authority considers appropriate.

After an entry has been made, a copy of the record must be served on the owner and occupier of the premises to which it relates and he may, within a twenty-eight day period from the service of the notice, then appeal to the Secretary of State. The Secretary of State may give such directions to the local authority as he thinks fit.

Except for this procedure, the validity or accuracy of an entry in the register cannot be questioned in any proceedings under this part of the Act. For example, in criminal proceedings, the court cannot consider the question of the accuracy of any recorded noise level. **s64**

Noise exceeding the registered level

The level of noise recorded in the register must not be exceeded without the written consent of the local authority. Consent can be given subject to conditions covering the amount by which the level may be exceeded and the period or periods when this may take place. Particulars of the consent must be kept in the noise level register.

If the authority does not give a decision within a two-month period from the receipt of the application for consent or such longer period as may be agreed, the authority will be deemed to have refused.

An applicant for consent may appeal against the authority's decision to the Secretary of State within three months from the date when the authority notified him of its decision. If the decision is a deemed refusal, the three months' period runs from the end of the two months' period or of an agreed extended period.

A consent issued under this section must contain a statement that it does not of itself constitute a defence to proceedings taken by an occupier of premises under s59.

If noise is emitted from premises in excess of the registered level without the consent of the local authority, or the terms of a consent to exceed the registered level are not observed, the person responsible will be guilty of an offence.

On conviction, a magistrate's court, if satisfied that the offence is likely to continue or recur, may make an order requiring works to be carried out to prevent this. Failure to comply with such an order is an offence.

Instead of, or in addition to, ordering the person convicted to carry out works, the court, after giving the local authority an opportunity to be heard, may order it to carry out the works. In addition, where a person fails to comply with an order requiring works, the local authority, on its own initiative, may carry them out. In either case the local authority can recover from the person in default the costs incurred in doing so, unless it can be shown that they were unnecessary. **s65**

Determination of registered level—new buildings

Where a building is going to be erected, or existing premises altered, and when built or altered a noise abatement order will apply to these premises, the local authority may, on the application of the owner or occupier or a person negotiating to acquire an interest in them, or on its own initiative, determine the level of noise from the premises which will be acceptable.

This level must be recorded in the register. Notification of the local authority's decision must be given to the applicant or, if it acts on its own initiative, to the owner or occupier of the premises. If within two months from the date when the local authority receives the application it fails to give a decision, it will be deemed to have declined to fix a noise level.

Where the authority fixes a level or notifies a refusal, the applicant or recipient may appeal to the Secretary of State within three months from the date of the notification. Where there is a deemed refusal, the applicant may appeal to the Secretary of State within three months from the end of the two-month period. **s67**

Appeals

Appeals can be made under s64 (recorded noise levels), s65 (consent to exceed the registered level) and s67 (noise level for new buildings).

The detailed procedure is contained in the Control of Noise (Appeals) Regulations 1975 (SI 1975 No 2116, para 9).

Notice of appeal must be made in writing and, within seven days of the giving of the notice or such longer period as the Secretary of State may allow, the following documents must be sent to him:

(a) The application, if any, made to the local authority.
(b) Any relevant plans and particulars submitted to the local authority.
(c) Any relevant record, consent, determination, notice or other notification issued by the authority.
(d) All other relevant correspondence with the authority.
(e) A plan of the premises concerned, unless one has already been submitted with any of the above documents.

The Secretary of State, if he thinks fit, may require the appellant or the local authority to submit within a specified period a further statement in writing concerning the subject matter of the appeal. If he then thinks that he is sufficiently informed, he may decide the appeal, but in any other case he must cause a local inquiry to be held.

When determining the appeal, the Secretary of State may allow or dismiss it, or reverse or vary any part of the record, consent, determination or decision of the local authority, or may deal with the application as if it had been made to him in the first instance.

At any time before the appeal is determined, the appellant may abandon it by giving written notice to the Secretary of State and then, as soon as possible, he must send a copy of it to the local authority.

Reduction of noise levels

The above provisions give local authorities powers to ensure that existing noise levels do not increase. They also have powers in some circumstances to reduce existing noise levels.

If in respect of premises subject to a noise abatement order the local authority thinks that the recorded noise level is not acceptable, having regard to the purpose for which the order was made, and that a reduction in the level is practicable at reasonable cost and would afford a public benefit, it may serve a noise reduction notice on the person responsible. This notice must require that person to reduce the level of noise coming from the premises to a specified level, to prevent any subsequent increase in the noise level without the local authority's consent, and to take specified steps to achieve these purposes. It must specify the time limit within which the noise must be reduced and within which any specified steps must be taken, which must not be less than six months from the date of service of the notice. It may specify particular times or days during which the noise level is to be reduced, and may require the level to be reduced to different levels for different times or days. Particulars of the notice must be recorded in the register.

A noise reduction notice is to take effect even though a consent to exceed the registered level issued under s65 authorises a noise level in excess of that specified in the notice.

Contravention of a noise reduction notice without reasonable excuse is an offence. However, where the noise is produced in the course of a trade or business, it is a defence to show that the best practicable means have been used to prevent or counteract its effect.

When the recipient of a noise reduction notice fails to carry out any specified works, the local authority may carry them out itself and recover the costs from the person in default, except such expenditure as can be shown to be unnecessary.

A person served with a noise reduction notice may, within three months from the date of service, appeal to a magistrate's court. **s66**

The details are contained in the Control of Noise (Appeals) Regulations 1975 (SI 1975 No 2116, para 7).

The grounds of appeal against a noise reduction notice may include such of the following as may be appropriate:

(a) That the notice is not justified in the terms of s66.
(b) That there has been some informality, defect or error in or in connection with the notice.
(c) That the authority has unreasonably refused to accept compliance with alternative requirements, or that the requirements of the notice are otherwise unreasonable in character or extent, or are unnecessary.
(d) That any time limit specified in the notice is not sufficient.
(e) That the best practicable means have been used to prevent or counteract the noise when produced in the course of a trade or business.
(f) That the notice should have been served on some person other than the appellant, being the person responsible for the noise.
(g) That the notice might lawfully have been served on some person in addition to the appellant, being a person also responsible for the noise, and that it would have been equitable for it to have been so served.

Where the appeal is under (g), the appellant must serve a copy of the notice of appeal on any person referred to, and in the case of an appeal on any grounds, he may serve a copy of the notice of appeal on anyone having an interest in the premises in question.

Where the appeal is under (b), the court must dismiss it if it is satisfied that the defect, informality or error was not material. In any other case the court may quash the notice, dismiss the appeal, or vary the notice in favour of the appellant in such a manner as it thinks fit. Such a varied notice is final, and shall have effect as if originally made in that form by the local authority.

The court may also make such an order as it thinks fit with respect to the person by whom any works are to be done, the contributions to be made by any person towards the cost of such works, and the proportions in which any expenses recoverable by the local authority are to be borne by the appellant and any other person. However, before making an order imposing any requirement on a person other than the appellant, the court must be satisfied that he has received a copy of the notice of appeal.

New buildings

Where a noise abatement order is in force, and premises become premises to which the order applies, either as the result of the construction of a building or as the result of operations carried out on those premises, and no noise level in respect of the premises has ben determined under s67 above, a local authority may serve a noise reduction notice.

In this case the above provisions apply, but with three modifications. The requirements that the reduction in noise level must be practicable and at a reasonable cost and that it would afford a public benefit are not applicable. The only matter to be considered by the local authority is whether the level of noise coming from the premises is unacceptable, having regard to the purposes for which the order was made.

Such a noise reduction notice may come into force after three months from the date of service, not six months.

In proceedings for a contravention of a noise reduction notice where the noise was caused in the course of a trade or business, it will not be a defence to prove that the best practicable means had been used to prevent or counteract the effect of the noise. **s67**

Miscellaneous Provisions

Suspension of notices pending an appeal

The Control of Noise (Appeals) Regulations 1975 (SI 1975 No 2116, para 10) deal with the question of the suspension of notices pending an appeal. Under these regulations the basic provision is that a notice will not be suspended by reason only of an appeal to a magistrate's court or to the Secretary of State.

A notice will be suspended in certain circumstances. Where the notice has been served under s58 (a noise nuisance), under s60 (a noise level on a construction site), or under s66 (a noise reduction notice), and the noise is caused in the course of the performance of a duty imposed by law, or if compliance would involve some person in the expense of carrying out works before the appeal is heard, the notice will be suspended.

However, even if the notice satisfies these requirements, it will not be suspended if in the local authority's opinion the noise is injurious to health or is likely to be of such a limited duration that suspension would have no practical effect, or that the expenditure would not be disproportionate compared with the expected benefit to the public during that period. The notice must contain a statement that it will take effect notwithstanding any appeal to a magistrate's court.

Codes of practice

The Secretary of State may, by order, prepare and issue codes of practice or approve codes of practice issued by other bodies for the purpose of giving guidance on appropriate methods for minimising noise, including the use of specified plant or machinery. This power has been exercised in relation to the control of noise on construction sites.

Any such order which issues or approves a code of practice may be varied or revoked by a subsequent order. **s71**

Best practicable means

Frequent mention is made of the defence of the use of the best practicable means. This is amplified in s72.

'Practicable' means reasonably practicable, having regard among other things to local conditions and circumstances, to the current state of technical knowledge, and to the financial implications. 'Means' include the design, installation, maintenance and manner and period of operation of plant and machinery, and the design, construction and maintenance of buildings and acoustic structures.

Regard must also be had to safety and safe working conditions, any duty imposed by law, and the exigencies of any emergency or unforeseen situation. Consideration must also be given to the relevant provisions of any approved code of practice. **s72**

Noise from plant or machinery

The Secretary of State may make regulations to require the use on, or in connection with, any plant or machinery of devices or arrangements for reducing the noise from that plant or machinery. Regulations may also be made to limit the amount of noise which may be caused by any plant or machinery used for works on construction sites, etc, (s60) or which may be caused outside a factory within the meaning of the Factories Act 1961 by the use of plant or machinery within it. Standards, specifications, descriptions and tests may be applied by the regulations although laid down in documents which do not form part of them.

Before the Secretary of State exercises his powers to make such regulations, he must consult persons representing the users and producers of plant or machinery to ensure that the regulations do not contain requirements which would be impracticable or involve unreasonable expense.

Different regulations may be made for different areas, and the local authority must enforce such regulations in its area.

Contravention of the regulations or permitting another person to contravene them is an offence. In proceedings for a contravention of regulations requiring the use on, or in connection with, plant or machinery of devices or arrangements to reduce the noise from it, it will be a defence to prove that alternative means were used which were not less effective than the means required by the regulations.

Any requirement imposed by such regulations will be in addition to and not instead of any of the other requirements, etc, contained in this part of the Act. However, currently no such regulations have been made. **s68**

Offences and Penalties

Joint offenders

Where more than one person is responsible for noise, the controls in this part of the Act apply to them individually, whether or not what any one of them was doing would by itself amount to a nuisance or result in a noise level justifying action under the Act. **s73(3)**

Penalties

The maximum penalties which can be imposed for an offence under this part of the Act are, on summary conviction for a first offence, a fine of £200, and for a second or subsequent offence, a fine of £400. In addition, in any case a further fine of not more than £50 per day on which the offence continues after conviction can be imposed.

In determining whether an offence is a further or subsequent offence, an offence under s95 of the Public Health Act 1936 will be treated as being an offence under this part of the Act, ie, contravention of a nuisance order relating to noise made under the 1936 Act and the Noise Abatement Act 1960. **s74**

Enforcement

The powers contained in the Control of Pollution Act are available to enforce these provisions (see p 156).

CHAPTER FIVE

THE CONTROL OF
ATMOSPHERIC POLLUTION

The aspect of the common law which will be of most relevance to atmospheric pollution is nuisance (see Chapter 1), and many of the most important cases on this subject are concerned with this problem.

The statutory control of air pollution goes back to 1863 when the first Alkali Act was passed following an inquiry into the alkali manufacturing industry which was causing large amounts of hydrogen chloride to be discharged into the atmosphere. Subsequent amendments were consolidated in the Alkali etc Works Regulation Act 1906, parts of which are still in force. The scheme of this legislation is that it controls specified emissions from premises of a specified class. These can broadly be described as chemical pollutants from industrial premises. Eventually these will be dealt with under the Health and Safety at Work Act 1974, parts of which are already applicable.

In addition to this legislation, a separate set of statutory provisions deriving from public health legislation and dealing with clean air and smoke generally is now contained in the Clean Air Acts and the Control of Pollution Act 1974.

A. THE ALKALI ETC WORKS REGULATION ACT 1906 AND THE HEALTH AND SAFETY AT WORK ACT 1974

The Alkali etc Works Regulation Act 1906

Under the Alkali Act 1906, enforcement was the responsibility of the Alkali Inspectorate who used the machinery contained in the Act for enforcement. This is now dealt with by the Health and Safety at Work Act 1974.

Before examining the legislation in detail, a short explanation of the 1974 Act is necessary. It is based on the recommendations of the Robens Committee on Safety and Health at Work. One of its main proposals was the replacement of the existing legislation on health and safety at work by a system of regulations and codes of practice issued under a single enabling Act. Section 1 of the Act states that the basic aims of the legislation are:

(a) To secure the health, safety and welfare of persons at work.
(b) To protect persons other than persons at work against risks to health or safety arising out of or in connection with the activities of persons at work.
(c) To control the use of explosive, inflammable or otherwise dangerous substances.
(d) To control the emission into the atmosphere of noxious or offensive substances from premises of a prescribed class.

Section 1 is declaratory of the main purposes of the Act, and these are amplified by the imposition of general duties in ss2–9. For instance, s2 states that it is the duty of every employer, so far as is reasonably practicable, to ensure the health, safety and welfare at work of all his employees.

In connection with air pollution, the important section is s5 which states that it is the duty of the person having control of any premises of a prescribed class to use the best practicable means for preventing the emission of noxious or offensive substances into the atmosphere and for rendering them harmless and inoffensive. However, this is qualified in that a person having control of premises is defined for these purposes as a person having control of premises in connection with carrying on a trade, business or undertaking, whether for profit or not, and any duty imposed on him extends only to matters within his control. 'Means' is defined as including the manner in which plant is used, and the supervision of activities involving the emission of substances to which the section applies.

It should be noted that 'prescribed' means prescribed in regulations. Thus, s5 will only apply to premises of a class specified in regulations. Currently, no such regulations have been made, and so s5 has no practical effect. The existing controls are those contained in the Alkali Act. (Compare the manner in which the Alkali Act applies to scheduled works, ie, those specified in the First Schedule to the Act.)

One of the objectives of the Act is the eventual replacement of all the existing legislation by health and safety regulations and codes of practice. Consequently, an important definition and one on which much of the Act is based is that of 'relevant statutory provisions'. These include the provisions of the Act, any health and safety regulations made thereunder, and the existing statutory provisions which are those Acts, regulations and orders, including the Alkali Act, which will eventually be replaced.

The enforcement provisions of the 1974 Act are available for enforcing any of the relevant statutory provisions. This means that they may be used to enforce the remaining provisions of the Alkali Act.

Alkali Works

Alkali works are defined as works for the manufacture of sulphate of soda or sulphate of potash, or for the treatment of copper ores by common salt or other chlorides, whereby any sulphate is formed in which muriatic acid (hydrochloric acid) is evolved. Every alkali work must be so carried on so as to secure the condensation of the muriatic acid gas evolved to the extent of 95 per cent, and to such an extent that in each cubic foot of air, smoke or chimney gases escaping from the works into the atmosphere there is not more than one-fifth of a grain of muriatic acid. **s1** (A cubic foot is to be calculated at 60°F and 30 inches of barometric pressure. **s16**)

In addition, the best practicable means must be used to prevent the escape of noxious or offensive gases by the exit flue of any apparatus used in any process carried on in the works, to prevent their discharge into the atmosphere, whether directly or indirectly, and to render them harmless and inoffensive if they are discharged. Any muriatic acid gas which does not exceed the limit imposed by s1 is to be ignored for the purpose of this section. **s2**

Failure to comply with either of the above provisions is an offence.

112

Sulphuric Acid Works

Sulphuric acid works are defined as works in which the manufacture of sulphuric acid is carried on by the lead chamber process in which sulphurous acid is converted to sulphuric acid by oxides of nitrogen and the use of a lead chamber, or by any other process involving the use of oxides of nitrogen. Such works must be so carried on as to secure the condensation of the acid gases of sulphur or of sulphur and nitrogen to the extent that the total acidity of those gases in each cubic foot (see above) of residual gases before mixing with air, smoke or chimney gases does not exceed the equivalent of four grains of sulphuric anhydride. **s6(1)**

Failure to comply with this provision is an offence.

Muriatic Acid Works

Muriatic acid works are defined as muriatic acid works, or works not being alkali works where muriatic acid gas is evolved either during the preparation of liquid muriatic acid or for use in any manufacturing process, or as the result of the use of chlorides in any chemical process; or tinplate flux works, ie, works where any residue or flux from tinplate works is calcined for the utilisation of such residue or flux and in which muriatic acid gas is evolved; or salt works, ie, works where the extraction of salt from brine is carried on and where muriatic acid gas is evolved.

These works must be carried on so as to secure the condensation of the muriatic acid gas evolved to the extent that in each cubic foot (see under Alkali Works) of air, smoke or chimney gases escaping into the atmosphere from such works there is not more than one-fifth of a grain of muriatic acid. **s6(2)**

Failure to comply with this provision is an offence.

Scheduled Works

Section 7 is by far the most important section of the 1906 Act. It applies to scheduled works, that is, those contained in the First Schedule to the Act which include sulphuric acid works and muriatic acid works, but not alkali works.

The Schedule has been amended several times, and currently contains over sixty sorts of works. It is impossible to generalise on the types of works, but they include works connected with the oil industry, iron and steel works, works connected with the chemical industry, gas works, power stations, potteries, and works involving

113

various metals such as aluminium, copper, lead, and zinc. For a complete list reference should be made to the First Schedule to the 1906 Act as amended.

The owner of any scheduled works must use the best practicable means to prevent the escape of noxious or offensive gases by the exit flue of any apparatus used in any process carried on in the works, to prevent the discharge, whether directly or indirectly of such gases into the atmosphere, and to render such gases where discharged harmless and inoffensive. However, to be ignored for the purpose of deciding whether an offence has been committed are any discharges of muriatic acid gas into the atmosphere where the amount discharged does not exceed one-fifth of a grain per cubic foot (see under Alkali Works) of air, smoke or gas, and acid gases from works for the concentration or distillation of sulphuric acid discharged into the atmosphere, where the total acidity of such gases does not exceed the equivalent of one and a half grains of sulphuric anhydride per cubic foot (see under Alkali Works, above) of air. **s7**

The definition of 'noxious or offensive gas' is contained in s27 as amended and, like the list of works to which the section applies, this is a long and complicated list. Reference should be made to the Act for details, but examples of gases within the definition are chlorine, fluorine, acid gases, ammonia, iodine, carbon monoxide, and fumes containing metals or their compounds.

In general, smoke, dust and grit are controlled by the Clean Air Acts, enforced by local authorities. However, for works subject to the Alkali Act, 'noxious or offensive gases' include smoke, dust and grit, and the Clean Air Acts do not apply to such works.

The test of the best practicable means to be applied includes not only the provision and maintenance of appliances to prevent an escape, but also the manner of use of such appliances and the supervision of the works in which the gases are evolved.

The owner of a works to which this section applies who fails to use the best practicable means to prevent the escape of any of the gases to which the section applies will be guilty of an offence.

Registration

Every scheduled works and alkali works must be registered, and a certificate of registration must be in force. This certificate is valid for one year from the date of the expiry of the previous certificate. If there was no previous certificate, the first certificate remains valid until the following 1 April. An application for a first registration may be made at any time, and the application for a renewal must be made in January or February.

Under the Alkali etc Works (Registration) Order 1957 (SI 1957 No 2208), the details to be included in an application and in the register are:

(a) The nature of the work.
(b) The name and postal address of the premises where the work is, or will be, carried on.
(c) The name of the owner and his business address if different from the address of the premises.
(d) The name of the local authority in whose area the premises are situated.
(e) The date when the works was erected.

Application must be made by or on behalf of the owner to the Health and Safety Executive.

Where the application is for first registration or for the registration of a works which has been closed for the previous twelve months, a certificate must not be issued unless the works is provided with such appliances as will enable work to be carried on in accordance with the requirements of the Act.

Where there is a change of ownership during the currency of a certificate or an alteration in any of the registered particulars, details must be sent to the Health and Safety Executive within one month. The certificate will be altered free of charge by an endorsement of the alteration. If a notice is not sent, the works will be deemed to be unregistered.

The owner of a works operated in contravention of these provisions is guilty of an offence. **s9**

Statutory Nuisances

As has been mentioned, proceedings in respect of statutory nuisances under the Public Health Act 1936 can be brought by a local authority, but unless the Secretary of State gives his consent it may not institute proceedings in respect of such a nuisance resulting from an accumulation, dust or effluvia if proceedings could be brought under the 1906 Act.

Metrication

Under the Control of Pollution Act 1974, the Secretary of State has power to make regulations to substitute amounts specified in metric units for amounts specified in other units. Any such amendments must preserve the effect of the original provisions, except that minor amendments can be made to obtain convenient and suitable amounts in metric units. **CPA s103**

The Health and Safety at Work Act 1974

Control over emissions from works subject to the Alkali Act will eventually come totally under the 1974 Act. Until then, the various duties laid down by the 1906 Act and outlined above remain in force as the substantive provisions, but are to be enforced by the relevant parts of the 1974 Act.

It should be noted that the enforcement provisions set out below apply to all the legislation contained in or covered by the 1974 Act, and not only to the Alkali Act and and s5.

The Health and Safety Commission and Executive

These two bodies were established by the 1974 Act.

The Commission has between six and nine members, and includes representatives of employers, employees and other bodies concerned with matters relating to the general purposes of this Act. It is subject to the overall supervision of the Secretary of State, and its functions are concerned with the formulation of policy to achieve the objectives of the Act, in particular by giving assistance to persons involved, encouraging education and research, and preparing proposals for regulations.

The Executive consists of three people, and is the body responsible for the enforcement of the Act and other relevant legislation.

Health and Safety Regulations

The existing legislation will be replaced by regulations made under the 1974 Act. These will be made by the Secretary of State who has very wide powers. He may act independently, or on the basis of recommendations submitted to him by the Commission. However, where he proposes to act independently, he must first consult the Commission and other interested bodies. The Commission must also be consulted where he proposes to modify recommendations. Where the Commission makes a recommendation, it must consult any interested Government department or other body which it considers appropriate, and such bodies as the Secretary of State may direct.

Regulations made under these provisions are called health and safety regulations and may be made for the following purposes:

(a) To repeal or modify existing statutory provisions.
(b) To exclude or modify the existing statutory provisions or the general duties in the 1974 Act in prescribed cases.
(c) To specify persons or authorities responsible for the enforcement of the relevant statutory provisions.
(d) To require the approval of the Commission or other specified body.
(e) To provide for references to documents in regulations to operate as references to revised or reissued versions of such documents.
(f) To provide for exemptions either conditionally or unconditionally, and with or without a time limit, from any requirement or prohibition in the relevant statutory provision.
(g) To enable exemptions to be granted by a specified person or authority.
(h) To specify the persons or class of person who are to be guilty of an offence.
(i) To provide for specified defences to be available, either generally or in specific circumstances.
(j) To exclude trial on indictment for contraventions and to limit the punishments which can be imposed in those cases.

The above is the list of purposes for which regulations may be made. The possible contents of regulations are set out in Schedule 3, and the matters which are likely to be of most relevance to the problems of air pollution are the following. Regulations may:

(1) Regulate the use of any plant, or the carrying on of any process or operation.
(2) Impose requirements as to the design, construction, repair, maintenance and inspection of any plant.
(3) Prohibit the carrying on of any specified activity or the doing of any specified thing, except under the authority of and in accordance with the terms of the licence or with the consent of a specified authority, and make provision for the granting, renewal, variation and transfer of licences.
(4) Require any person, premises or thing to be registered in specified circumstances, or as a condition of carrying on a specified activity or doing a specified thing.
(5) Prohibit or impose requirements in connection with the emission into the atmosphere of specified gas, smoke or dust or other specified substance, and impose requirements as to the monitoring of such emissions.

(6) Impose requirements as to the instruction, training and supervision of persons at work.
(7) Require specified matters to be notified to specified persons, and empower inspectors to require written statements of measures proposed to be taken to ensure compliance with any of the relevant statutory provisions.
(8) Impose requirements as to the keeping of records and other documents.
(9) Restrict, prohibit or require the doing of any specified thing where there has been an accident or occurrence of a specified kind. **s15,** Schedule 3

Codes of Practice

The Commission may approve and issue codes of practice or approve codes of practice issued by other persons to provide practical guidance with respect to the general duties imposed by the Act, health and safety regulations, or the existing statutory provisions.

Before approving a code of practice, the Commission must consult any Government department or other body it considers appropriate and such department or other body as the Secretary of State has directed. After such consultation, the approval of the Secretary of State must be obtained.

Where the Commission has approved a code of practice, a notice must be issued specifying the code, the date on which the approval is to take effect, and the statutory provision to which it applies.

The Commission may revise a code of practice it has issued, or approve a revision to a code issued by another person, and may withdraw its approval from a code of practice. Similar requirements of consultation and publicity are applicable to a withdrawal or a variation of a code.

Contravention of an approved code of practice does not of itself render any person liable to civil or criminal proceedings. However, a code of practice is admissible in evidence. Where there are criminal proceedings in respect of an alleged breach of a statutory provision in respect of which there is in force an approved code of practice, and it is proved that at any material time there was a failure to observe any relevant part of the code of practice, the defendant will be liable unless he can satisfy the court that the relevant statutory provision was complied with in some other way. **ss16–17**

Enforcement

Authorities

The responsibility for the day-to-day enforcement of the Act is placed on the Executive under which the Alkali Inspectorate now enforces the 1906 Act. The Secretary of State may make a local authority responsible for the enforcement of specified statutory provisions. The Executive and these local authorities are together called enforcing authorities. **s18**

Appointment of inspectors

Each enforcing authority may appoint such inspectors as it thinks necessary to ensure that the relevant statutory provisions for which it is responsible are complied with. The appointment of an inspector must be in writing, and must specify which of the powers he may exercise.

An inspector is only allowed to exercise these specified powers, but if he acts outside them, honestly believing that what he did was within his powers and that his duty required or entitled him to take such action, the authority which appointed him may indemnify him, although not legally obliged to do so. When exercising or seeking to exercise his powers, an inspector must, if requested, produce his instrument of appointment or a certified copy. **s19**

Powers of inspectors

Subject to any limitations set out in his appointment, an inspector may exercise any of the following powers for the enforcement of any of the relevant statutory provisions which are the responsibility of the authority which appointed him. An inspector may:

(a) At any reasonable time, or at any time if he thinks there is or may be an emergency, enter premises.
(b) Take with him a constable if he has reasonable cause to apprehend a serious obstruction in the execution of his duty.
(c) Take with him any other person authorised by the authority which appointed him, and any equipment or materials required for any purpose for which the power of entry is being exercised.
(d) Make such examination and investigations as may be necessary.
(e) Direct that any premises or any part shall be left undisturbed for as long as is necessary for the purpose of an investigation or examination.

(f) Take such measurements, photographs and recordings as he considers necessary.

(g) Take samples of any articles or substances in the premises or samples of the atmosphere in or in the vicinity of the premises. Regulations may be made to lay down the procedure to be followed in connection with the taking of samples, including the way in which they are to be taken.

(h) In the case of any article or substance likely to cause danger to health or safety, cause it to be dismantled or subjected to any process or test but not so as to damage or destroy it, unless this is necessary for the purpose of exercising his powers. If the person responsible for the premises so requests, the inspector must exercise these powers in the presence of that person unless he considers that it would be prejudicial to the safety of the State. Before exercising these powers, an inspector must consult such persons as he considers appropriate to ascertain what dangers there might be in what he proposes to do.

(i) In the case of such an article or substance as is mentioned in (h) above, he may take possession of it and detain it for so long as is necessary to examine it, to ensure that it is not tampered with and that it is available for use in any legal proceedings. The inspector must leave a notice either with a responsible person or fixed at a conspicuous place to the effect that he has taken the substance or article, and he must if practicable leave a sample with a responsible person.

(j) If conducting an examination or investigation under (d) require any person who he thinks can give any relevant information to answer questions and sign a declaration as to the truth of the answers.

(k) Require the production of, inspect and take copies of any books or documents which must be kept under any of the relevant statutory provisions, and any other books or documents which it is necessary for him to see for the purposes of his investigation.

(l) Require any person to give such facilities and assistance within that person's control or responsibility as are necessary to enable him to exercise any of his powers.

(m) Exercise any other power which is necessary. **s20**

Notices

Prohibition and improvement notices, important innovations introduced by the Act, give inspectors flexible powers to deal with breaches of the relevant statutory provisions.

Improvement notices

An improvement notice may be served by an inspector if he is of the opinion that someone is contravening one or more of the relevant statutory provisions, or has contravened them in circumstances which make it likely that the breach will be continued or repeated.

This notice must state that this is the inspector's opinion, specify the provision or provisions in question, and require the person to remedy the contravention within a specified period which must be not less than the period within which an appeal may be made—currently twenty-one days. **s21**

Prohibition notices

A prohibition notice can be served on the person in control of an activity by an inspector if he is of the opinion that the activity is or will be if carried out, subject to the relevant statutory provisions and involves or will involve a risk of serious personal injury.

This notice must state that this is the inspector's opinion, and must specify the matters which give rise to or will give rise to the risk. Where, in his opinion, a contravention of any of the relevant statutory provisions is also involved, the notice must state this, specify the relevant provision or provisions, and give particulars of his reasons. The notice must also direct that the activities must not be carried on until the specified matters and any contravention have been remedied. If the notice states that the risk of serious injury is imminent, then the notice has immediate effect. In any other case, the notice has effect at the end of the period specified in the notice. **s22**

Notices—miscellaneous provisions

A prohibition notice or an improvement notice may, but need not, include directions as to the measures to be taken to remedy any matter or contravention. These directions may be made by reference to an approved code of practice, and may give the person to whom a notice is addressed a choice of different measures to be taken.

In respect of a building to which a relevant statutory provision applies, an improvement notice cannot impose requirements more onerous than those which could be imposed by Building Regulations if the building were newly erected, unless the statutory provision itself imposes more onerous requirements.

An improvement notice, or a prohibition notice not having immediate effect, can be withdrawn by an inspector at any time before the date on which it comes into effect. The period before it becomes effective can be extended or further extended by an inspector at any time when an appeal against the notice is not pending. **s23**

Appeals against notices

A person on whom a notice has been served may appeal against it to an industrial tribunal within such period from its date of service as may be specified—currently twenty-one days. On appeal, the tribunal may cancel or affirm the notice, and, if it affirms it, it may do so in its original form or with modifications.

Where there is an appeal against an improvement notice, the effect of the notice will be suspended pending the determination or withdrawal of the appeal.

Where there is an appeal against a prohibition notice, it will only be suspended if the appellant applies for suspension to an industrial tribunal and the tribunal so directs. If it does, the suspension only has effect from the date of the tribunal's direction.

Where appropriate, one or more assessors may be appointed to an industrial tribunal for the purpose of proceedings under these provisions. **s24**

Investigations and Inquiries

Where there is an accident, occurrence, situation or other matter which the Commission thinks should be investigated for any of the general purposes of the Act or with a view to making regulations, it can direct the Executive or authorise any other person to investigate and make a special report. Alternatively, it may, with the consent of the Secretary of State, direct an inquiry to be held. This must be conducted in accordance with regulations, and be in public unless the regulations provide otherwise. The Commission may authorise the publication of the whole or part of a report made as the result of an investigation or inquiry. **s14**

Information

The Commission, with the consent of the Secretary of State, may serve a notice on any person requiring him to furnish information on specified matters which the Commission or an enforcing authority requires for the discharge of its functions. The Secretary of State may give a general consent to cases of a stated description.

Under the Statistics of Trade Act 1947, Government departments have powers to require information, but there are restrictions on the disclosure of this. However, disclosure to the Commission and the Executive by Government departments is not subject to the restrictions in the 1947 Act, but such information as is disclosed can only be used for the purposes of the Executive and Commission. **s27**

Restrictions on the disclosure of information obtained as a result of notices or of any requirement imposed by any of the relevant statutory provisions are contained in the 1974 Act. Generally speaking, no one who obtains such information may disclose it without the consent of the person from whom it was obtained.

However, there are exceptions. The recipient of the information may disclose it to the Commission, the Executive, a Government department or an enforcing authority. It may be disclosed for the purpose of any function conferred on the recipient by any relevant statutory provision, and it may be given to authorised officials of a local authority or a water authority, or to a constable authorised by his Chief Constable to receive it. It may also be disclosed for the purpose of legal proceedings, an investigation or inquiry or the report of an investigation or inquiry, or a special report.

The person to whom such information is given may only use it in connection with the responsibilities of the authority or other body concerning such matters as the relevant statutory provisions, Acts relating to public health, the protection of the environment, or the safety of the State.

A person conducting an investigation or inquiry who obtains information, or an inspector who acquires information during the exercise of his powers, in particular information relating to a trade secret, may only disclose it in the exercise of his functions, in connection with legal proceedings, an investigation or inquiry, or a report or a special report, or with the consent of the person who furnished the information.

Finally, information may be disclosed provided it cannot be identified as being applicable to a particular case. **s28**

Offences

Offences in connection with atmospheric pollution are:

(a) Failing to discharge a duty imposed by ss2–7, particularly s5.

(b) Contravening health and safety regulations, or any requirement or prohibition imposed under such regulations, including the terms of a condition or restriction attached to a licence or consent given or granted under the regulations.

(c) Contravening regulations made to govern the conduct of investigations or inquiries or obstructing any person in the exercise of his powers to conduct an investigation or inquiry.

(d) Contravening any requirement imposed by the inspector in the exercise of his powers.

(e) Preventing or attempting to prevent any person from appearing before an inspector or from answering any questions the inspector is empowered to ask.

(f) Contravening any requirement or prohibition imposed by an improvement notice or a prohibition notice.

(g) Intentionally obstructing an inspector in the exercise of his powers or duties.

(h) Contravening any requirement in a notice requiring information.

(i) Using or disclosing information in a manner not permitted by the Act.

(j) Deliberately or recklessly making a false statement either in connection with a requirement to furnish information or in connection with an application for the issue of any document under any of the relevant statutory provisions.

(k) Intentionally making a false entry in any record required to be kept by or under any of the relevant statutory provisions or, with intent to deceive, making use of such an entry known to be false.

(l) With intent to deceive, forging a document or using a forged document issued under any of the relevant statutory provisions.

(m) Failing to comply with an order of the court under s42 under which a court can order a person convicted of an offence to remedy the matter (see below).

(n) An offence under the existing statutory provisions, ie, for present purposes, a failure to comply with the duties contained in the Alkali Act. **s33**

Penalties

The maximum penalty which can be imposed under (c), (d), (e) and (g) above is a fine of £1000 on summary conviction.

Subject to any provisions in health and safety regulations restricting penalties, for other offences, including a contravention of the provisions of the Alkali Act, the maximum penalties are, on summary conviction, a fine of £400, and on conviction on indictment,

124

an unlimited fine, and in certain circumstances, two years' imprisonment.

Imprisonment is possible for:

(a) The contravention of any of the relevant statutory provisions by acting otherwise than under the authority of a licence issued by the Executive, where such a licence is necessary.
(b) Contravening the terms of such a licence.
(c) An offence under (f) above which consists of contravening a requirement or prohibition imposed by a prohibition notice.
(d) An offence under (i) above.

Where the offence is under (f) or (m) above and the contravention continues after conviction, the person responsible will be guilty of a further offence and subject to a maximum fine of £100 per day on which the offence continues after conviction. **s33**

When a person is convicted of an offence, and the court thinks that the matters in question can be remedied by him, it may order him to take specified steps to remedy the matters within a specified period in addition to or instead of imposing a penalty. The time limit may be extended or further extended by an application to the court before the end of the period as originally fixed or previously extended.

Where a person is ordered to remedy a matter, he will not be liable under any of the relevant statutory provisions in respect of that matter during the time fixed by the order or an extension. **s42**

Legal proceedings

Time limits

Under the Magistrate's Courts Act 1952, the rule relating to time limits for commencing proceedings can be summarised as follows. Unless otherwise provided, a magistrate's court cannot try a criminal offence unless proceedings are instituted within six months from the date when the offence was committed.

There are certain extensions to this period contained in the 1974 Act. Where there is a special report or a report is made after an inquiry, or there is an inquest into a death of which the cause was connected with work and it appears from the report or the proceedings that at a material time there was a contravention of any of the relevant statutory provisions, summary proceedings may begin at any time within the period of three months beginning with the date on which the report was made or the inquest was concluded.

Where an offence was committed by reason of failure to do something at a particular time or within a time limit, it is deemed to continue until that thing is done, and the time limit only begins to run from that time. **s34**

Offences due to the fault of another

Subject to any regulations, where a person commits an offence under any of the relevant statutory provisions by reason of the act or default of another, then that other person may be proceeded against and convicted whether or not proceedings are taken against the first person. **s36**

Corporations

Where an offence under any of the relevant statutory provisions is committed by a body corporate with the consent or connivance of, or is attributable to the neglect of, any director, manager, secretary, or other officer, then he, as well as the body corporate, will be guilty of the offence and liable to be proceeded against and punished. **s37**

Proceedings

Proceedings for an offence under any of the relevant statutory provisions can only be instituted by an inspector or with the consent of the Director of Public Prosecutions. An inspector may prosecute before a magistrate's court, although not qualified as a solicitor or a barrister. **ss38, 39**

Proof of practicability

Where an offence consists of a failure to do something insofar as it is practicable or a failure to use the best practicable means, the accused must prove that it was not practicable to do more or that there was no better practicable means than those he had adopted. **s40**

Civil Liability

A breach of the general duties contained in ss2–7 of the Health and Safety at Work Act does not give rise to any civil liability, nor does any provision of the 1974 Act affect any action for breach of statutory duty under the existing statutory provisions.

However, a breach of a duty imposed by health and safety regulations will involve civil liability insofar as such breach causes damage except to such extent as the regulations themselves exclude such liability.

Defences set down in regulations to criminal proceedings will not be available in civil proceedings, but the regulations themselves may prescribe defences available in civil proceedings. **s47**

Under the Alkali Act there is no provision for civil liability. The only remedy is that a local authority, as the result of information given by its officers or by any ten inhabitants of the district, may complain to the Health and Safety Executive that works to which the Act applies are being carried on in contravention of the Act and are causing a nuisance to the inhabitants of the district. The Executive must then investigate and may direct that proceedings be instituted. **s22/1906**

Apart from this, the general rule is that any provision for civil liability for breach of statutory duty does not affect any right of action which exists independently of the relevant Act.

B.   THE CLEAN AIR ACTS 1956 AND 1968 AND THE CONTROL OF POLLUTION ACT 1974

The Alkali Act and the Health and Safety at Work Act only apply to specified emissions from specified classes of premises. The controls over other forms of atmospheric pollution are to be found in public health legislation.

The Public Health Act 1936, in addition to applying the statutory nuisance provisions to dust and effluvia (which are still in force), also imposed controls on smoke nuisance. The current legislation is to be found in the Clean Air Acts 1956 and 1968, and the Control of Pollution Act 1974. The enforcing authorities for these Acts are local authorities, for this purpose, district councils.

The Clean Air Acts 1956 and 1968

Smoke

Dark smoke

It is an offence to emit dark smoke from a chimney of any building, or from a chimney serving the furnace of any boiler or industrial plant which is a boiler or plant attached to a building or fixed to or installed on land, or from any industrial or trade premises.

Dark smoke for this purpose is defined as smoke which would appear as dark as or darker than shade 2 on the Ringelman chart.

The maximum penalties for a contravention of this provision are, on summary conviction, a fine of £400 unless the smoke is emitted from the chimney of a private dwelling, when the maximum penalty is a fine of £100.

(This ban on the emission of dark smoke also applies to all vessels, basically those within UK territorial waters, and subject to a maximum fine of £100 on summary conviction.)

There are exceptions to this prohibition.

Emissions from chimneys

The Act provides four defences where an offence has been committed:

(a) That the contravention was due solely to the lighting up of a cold furnace and that all practicable steps were taken to prevent or minimise the emission of dark smoke.

(b) That the contravention was due solely to an unforeseeable failure of a furnace or apparatus used in connection with a furnace, or a foreseeable failure which could not reasonably have been provided against, and that the contravention could not reasonably have been prevented after the failure occurred.

(c) That the contravention was due solely to the use of an unsuitable fuel when no suitable fuel was available, that the least unsuitable fuel had been used, and that all practicable steps had been taken to prevent or minimise the emission of dark smoke.

(d) That the contravention was due to a combination of the above and that the conditions specified in respect of them all were satisfied.

In addition to these defences, the Dark Smoke (Permitted Periods) Regulations 1958 (SI 1958 No 498) provide that specified periods are not to be taken into account in deciding whether an offence has been committed.

Under these it is permitted to emit dark smoke for not longer than ten minutes in the aggregate in any eight hour period or, if soot-blowing is carried out in any such period, for not longer than fourteen minutes in the aggregate. These periods of ten and fourteen minutes are to be increased to eighteen and twenty-five minutes in the case of a chimney serving two furnaces. Where a chimney serves three furnaces, the increase is to twenty-four and thirty-four minutes, or where it serves four or more chimneys, the increase is to twenty-nine and forty-one minutes.

However, nothing is to authorise the continuous emission of dark smoke caused otherwise than by soot-blowing for any period exceeding four minutes, or the emission of black smoke (defined as as dark as or darker than shade 4 on the Ringelman chart) for more than two minutes in the aggregate in any period of thirty minutes.

Nothing in these exceptions is to apply to vessels.

Emissions from industrial or trade premises

It will be a defence to a charge of emitting dark smoke from such premises to prove that the emission was inadvertent, and that all practicable steps had been taken to prevent or minimise its emission.

In addition to this defence, the Clean Air (Emission of Dark Smoke) (Exemption) Regulations 1969 (SI 1969 No 1263) exempt dark smoke caused by the burning of prescribed matter. The exemption of most general application, although not the only one, is that of smoke from the burning of timber and any waste matter, other than rubber or feathers, resulting from the demolition of a building or clearance of a site in connection with any building operation or work of engineering construction. It is exempted provided that there was no other reasonably safe and practicable method of disposal, that steps were taken to minimise the emission of dark smoke, and that the burning was carried out under the supervision of the occupier of the premises or a person authorised to act on his behalf.

For other exceptions and the conditions applicable to them reference should be made to the regulations. **s1/56, s1/68**

Smoke from new furnaces

No furnace is to be installed in any building or in any boiler or industrial plant attached to a building unless, as far as practicable, it is capable of being operated continuously without emitting smoke when burning fuel of a type for which it was designed. This does not apply to a furnace which either was installed, or which it had been agreed would be purchased and installed, on 1 June 1958. Nor does it apply to furnaces designed solely or mainly for domestic purposes, provided the heating capacity does not exceed 55 000 BTU per hour.

A furnace must not be installed in a building, plant or boiler unless notice of the proposed installation has been given to the relevant local authority. Failure to give notice is a criminal offence with a maximum penalty on summary conviction of £100.

If plans are submitted to the local authority and approved for the purposes of this section, then it will be deemed to apply with the above requirements. It should be noted that approval under the

Building Regulations is not sufficient approval for this purpose. **s3/56**

Regulations

The Secretary of State has powers to make regulations to impose requirements as to the provision and installation of apparatus to indicate or record the density or darkness of any smoke emitted from a furnace, or to facilitate the observation of such smoke to ascertain its density or darkness. Regulations may also require chimneys serving furnaces to be adapted for these purposes. Requirements may be imposed as to the use and maintenance of apparatus provided under the regulations, and the making available to local authorities of any results recorded.

Contravention of these regulations will be an offence. Currently, none have been made. **s4/56**

Grit and Dust from Furnaces

Arrestment plant

The 1956 Act imposed requirements as to the use of arrestment plant for grit and dust in connection with certain furnaces. The 1968 Act extended these requirements. Now the controls of the 1956 Act only apply if the 1968 Act is not applicable.

These requirements apply equally to a furnace in a building and to a furnace attached to a boiler or industrial plant attached to a building or fixed or installed on land.

Under the 1956 Act, a furnace must not be used to burn pulverised fuel or other solid fuel or solid waste at the rate of one ton per hour or more, unless it is provided with plant for arresting grit or dust which has been approved by the local authority or which has been installed in accordance with plans submitted to and approved by the local authority, and the plant is properly maintained and used.

This requirement does not apply to a furnace which was installed, the installation of which had been begun, or an agreement for the purchase or installation of which had been entered into before 31 December 1956.

Failure to comply with this requirement is an offence.

The Secretary of State may direct that specified applications are to be referred to him for approval, and shall not be dealt with by local authorities.

The decision of the local authority must be in writing and, in the case of a refusal, reasons must be given. An applicant who is

130

dissatisfied with the decision of the local authority may appeal to the Secretary of State within twenty-eight days from the date when he was notified of the decision. **s6/56**

Under the 1968 Act, no furnace in which solid, liquid or gaseous matter is burnt, other than furnaces designed wholly or mainly for domestic purposes and used for heating a boiler with a maximum capacity of 55 000 BTU, shall be used to burn pulverised fuel, to burn any other solid matter at a rate of 100 lb per hour or more, or to burn any liquid or gaseous matter at a rate equivalent to 1.25 million BTU per hour or more, unless the furnace is fitted with an approved arrestment plant for grit and dust.

The procedure for approval, including appeal, is the same as under the 1956 Act. This requirement does not apply to a furnace which had been installed, the installation of which had been begun, or the agreement for the purchase or installation of which had been entered into before 1 October 1969.

Failure to comply with this requirement is an offence.

The Secretary of State has a power, not yet exercised, to reduce these rates of 100 lb per hour and 1.25 million BTU per hour by regulations which will require the approval of both Houses of Parliament. If there is such a reduction, the new regulations will not apply to a furnace which was installed, the installation of which had been begun, or an agreement for the purchase or installation of which had been entered into before the date when they came into force. **s3/68**

Exemptions

There are exemptions from the requirements to fit arrestment plant imposed by the 1968 Act, but not from those imposed by the 1956 Act. The exemptions fall into two categories, exemption by regulations and exemption granted by a local authority.

Exemption by regulations

The Secretary of State has the power to make regulations to exempt classes of furnaces while used for prescribed purposes. Details are to be found in the Clean Air (Arrestment Plant) (Exemption) Regulations 1969 (SI 1969 No 1262).

These exemptions can be summarised as mobile furnaces providing a temporary source of heat or power during building operations or engineering construction, for investigation or research, or for agricultural purposes. Also exempted are furnaces, other than those designed to burn solid matter at a rate of one ton per hour or more, in which the matter burnt does not contribute to the emission of grit and dust and which are included on the list contained in the regulations, when they are used for any purpose except the incineration of refuse.

Exemption by local authorities

A local authority may exempt a furnace from the requirements to fit an arrestment plant if the occupier of the premises applies and satisfies it that the emission of grit and dust would not be prejudicial to health or a nuisance if it were used for a particular purpose.

The above regulations prescribe the information which must be contained in an application, but a local authority may grant an exemption even if the requirements are not complied with exactly, provided that it is satisfied that it has received sufficient information. Briefly, the application must contain:

(a) The name and address of the applicant, details of the premises where the furnace is situated, and details of any consultant, contractor, or other agent.

(b) Details of the furnace, the purpose for which it is to be used, and the manner of operation.

(c) The grounds on which the exemption is sought, ie, it must be shown that the emission would not be prejudicial to health or a nuisance.

(d) The application must be signed and dated.

If the local authority fails to make and notify a decision within eight weeks from the date of receipt of the application or such longer period as may be agreed in writing, the furnace will be treated as if the exemption had been granted for the purpose set out in the application.

A written notification of the authority's decision and a statement of reasons must be given. If the authority refuses the exemption, the applicant has twenty-eight days from the date of the notification of the decision to appeal to the Secretary of State who may confirm the refusal, grant the exemption, or vary the purpose for which the furnace may be used without complying with the requirements. The Secretary of State must give the appellant a written notification of his decision, together with a statement of his reasons.

If, on any day, a furnace is used for a purpose other than one specified in regulations or contained in an exemption, the occupier of the building will be guilty of an offence. **s4/68**

Limits on emissions of grit and dust

The Secretary of State has power to make regulations prescribing limits to the rates of emission of grit and dust from furnaces in which any solid, liquid or gaseous matter is burnt, except those designed wholly or mainly for domestic purposes and used for heating boilers with a maximum capacity of less than 55 000 BTU per hour.

If grit or dust is emitted in excess of the limit on any day, the occupier of the premises will be guilty of an offence. It is a defence to prove that the best practicable means had been used to minimise the emission. If no limit is fixed, failure to use the best practicable means to minimise the emission of dust or grit will be an offence.

The Clean Air (Emission of Grit and Dust from Furnaces) Regulations 1971 (SI 1971 No 162), which were made for this purpose, came into force on 1 November 1971. These apply to all furnaces of the relevant rating, whenever constructed. The transitional provisions, exempting furnaces installed on 1 November 1971, came to an end on 31 December 1977.

Reference should be made to the regulations for details, but the basic scheme is that the maximum quantity of grit or dust which can be emitted per hour is to be ascertained by reference to the heat input or output of the furnace. **s2/68**

Measurement of grit and dust

Where a furnace is used to burn pulverised fuel or other solid matter at a rate of 100 lb per hour or more, or to burn at a rate of 1.25 million BTU per hour or more any liquid or gaseous matter, the local authority may serve on the occupier of the premises where the furnace is situated a notice that the following requirements apply to that furnace. Such a notice can be revoked by a subsequent notice but without prejudice to the authority's right to serve a further notice.

It should be noted that the rates mentioned above may be reduced by regulations which will require the approval of both Houses of Parliament. Currently, no such regulations have been made.

The requirements are such matters as the Secretary of State may specify in regulations for:

(a) The purpose of making and recording measurements of the grit, dust and fumes emitted:

(b) The adaptation of a chimney for that purpose.

(c) The provision and maintenance of apparatus.

(d) The taking of recordings.

(e) The furnishing of information to the local authority.

Under the Clean Air (Measurement of Grit and Dust from Furnaces) Regulations 1971 (SI 1971 No 161), the authority must give at least six weeks' notice of its requirements to the occupier. Within that period the occupier must make such adaptions to the chimney as are necessary to enable one of the methods in BS 3405:1961 to be used, and must provide the relevant apparatus which must be maintained in good working order.

Once this has been done, the occupier, on receiving at least twenty-eight days' notice, must take the required measurements and recordings within the specified period. At least forty-eight hours' notice of the date and time at which it is proposed to commence the measurements must be given to the local authority.

A record must be kept in respect of each chimney, and this must contain the date when the recordings were made, the number of furnaces discharging to the chimney, the measurement in lb per hour of grit and dust emitted, and the percentage of grit in the emitted solids. A copy of the results must be sent within fourteen days to the local authority.

A notice served by a local authority may require the taking of measurements from time to time at stated intervals, but an occupier cannot be required to take measurements in respect of a chimney more than once in a three month period, unless, in the opinion of the local authority, the true level of grit and dust cannot be ascertained without further measurements. A representative of the local authority is entitled to be present when these measurements are made.

If the furnace is used to burn solid matter other than pulverised fuel at a rate of less than one ton per hour or to burn liquid or gaseous matter at a rate of less than 28 million BTU per hour the occupier may, by notice, require the local authority to take the measurements and recordings. If the occupier serves such a notice, which can be revoked subsequently, then the local authority is obliged to take the measurements and recordings, and the occupier is not obliged to comply with any of the requirements except those relating to the adaptation of the chimney so that readings can be made. A notice sent by a local authority imposing these requirements must contain a statement of this right. **s7/56, s5/68**

Power to obtain information

To enable a local authority to perform its duty under the preceding provisions relating to grit and dust, it may serve a notice on the occupier of any building requiring him to furnish within fourteen days or a specified longer period such information as to the furnaces in the building and the fuel or waste burned as may reasonably be required.

Failure to comply with such a notice, or knowingly to give information which is false in a material particular, is an offence. **s8/56**

Chimneys

The 1956 Act imposed controls over chimneys but, as a result of the 1968 Act, the 1956 Act now applies only to chimneys not serving furnaces. Chimneys serving furnaces are now under the more extensive controls in the 1968 Act.

The 1956 Act

Where plans for the erection of a building outside the Inner London boroughs, other than plans for residences, shops or offices, are, in accordance with Building Regulations, deposited with a local authority, and they show that it is proposed to build a chimney to carry away smoke, dust or gases from the building, the authority must reject them unless it is satisfied that the height of the chimney as shown on the plans will be sufficient to prevent, so far as is practicable, these emissions from becoming prejudicial to health or a nuisance. The authority must take into account the purpose of the chimney, the position and description of nearby buildings, the levels of neighbouring ground and any other relevant matters.

If the plans are rejected, any person interested in the building may appeal to the Secretary of State who may confirm or cancel the rejection. If the rejection is cancelled he may, if he thinks necessary, direct that the time within which the plans may be rejected for other reasons shall be extended to run from the date on which his decision is notified to the local authority.

Where the local authority rejects plans on these grounds, the notice must specify that the above is the reason for the rejection. **s10/56**

The 1968 Act

Under the 1968 Act the controls are similar, but more extensive.

It is an offence to cause or permit to be used a furnace which burns pulverised fuel or other solid matter at a rate in excess of 100 lb per hour, or burns liquid or gaseous matter at a rate equivalent to 1.25 million or more BTU per hour, unless the height of the chimney serving the furnace has been approved and any conditions attached to the approval are complied with. Approval is necessary for a new chimney, a furnace where the combustion space is increased, and a furnace which replaces one with a smaller combustion space.

An application must be made to the local authority and must contain prescribed details, but even if this prescribed form is not followed the authority can give approval if satisfied that enough information has been given.

These details are contained in the Clean Air (Height of Chimneys) (Prescribed Form) Regulations 1969 (SI 1969 No 412), and must include:

(a) The name and address of the applicant.
(b) The address of the premises.
(c) The name and address of any contractor, consultant or agent.
(d) The category under which approval is sought.

Details must also be submitted of the furnaces, the fuel, the emissions, the buildings, the chimney and other relevant matters.

The local authority must not grant approval unless satisfied that the height will be sufficient to prevent, as far as is practicable, the smoke, dust or fumes from becoming prejudicial to health or a nuisance. The authority must take into consideration the purpose of the chimney, the position and description of any nearby buildings, the levels of neighbouring ground and any other relevant matters.

Approval may be given without qualification or subject to conditions as to the rate and/or quality of the emissions from the chimney. If the local authority fails to determine the application within four weeks from the date when it was received, or such longer period as may be agreed in writing, approval will be deemed to have been given without qualification.

If a local authority does not give approval, or gives approval subject to conditions, it must give a written statement of its decision and the reasons for it. If there is a refusal to approve the height of the chimney, it must specify the lowest height it would approve unconditionally or the lowest height it would approve subject to specified conditions, or both.

136

The applicant may appeal to the Secretary of State against the refusal or against the approval subject to conditions within twenty-eight days of receiving the notification.

The Secretary of State may confirm the local authority's decision, may approve the height of the chimney with or without conditions as to the rate and/or quality of the emissions, may cancel any conditions, or may substitute for the conditions imposed by the local authority any conditions which the authority could have imposed. A written notification of the decision must be given, stating the reasons for it and, if the decision is not to approve the height of the chimney, it must specify the lowest height, if any, which would be approved without qualification or the lowest height which would be approved subject to specified conditions, or both.

It is also an offence to use a furnace of a boiler or industrial plant attached to a building or for the time being fixed to or installed on land to burn pulverised fuel, other solid matter, liquid or gaseous matter at the rates specified above unless the height of the chimney has been approved and any conditions are complied with. Exceptions are contained in the Clean Air (Height of Chimneys) (Exemption) Regulations 1969 (SI 1969 No 411). The most important are that a boiler or plant will be exempt if it is being used as a temporary replacement for any other boiler or plant being inspected, repaired, maintained, rebuilt, or replaced by a permanent boiler or plant, or if it is being used as a temporary source of power or heat during building works, works of engineering construction, for investigation or research, or to heat other plant to an operating temperature. **s6/68**

Fumes

The Secretary of State can extend the controls over grit and dust to include fumes, and the requirement that new furnaces should be smokeless to apply to fumes as well as smoke. This power is to be exercised by regulations which need the consent of both Houses of Parliament. Currently, no such regulations have been made. **s7/68**

Smoke Control Areas

Designation

By order confirmed by the Secretary of State, a local authority may declare the whole or any part of its district to be a smoke control area. The procedure to be followed is contained in the First Schedule to the 1956 Clean Air Act.

After the local authority has made the order, it must publish a notice in the London Gazette and once at least in each of two successive weeks in a newspaper circulating in the area to which the order relates. This notice must state that an order has been made, and specify a place where a copy of the order and any map or plan may be inspected by any person, free of charge, at all reasonable times, during a period of not less than six weeks from the date of the last publication of the notice. It must also state that any person who will be affected by the order may, within that specified period, object to the Secretary of State against confirmation of the order. Copies of the notice must also be posted at conspicuous places in the area to which the notice relates.

If no objection is made, or if objections have been withdrawn, the Secretary of State may confirm the order with or without modifications. In any other case he must, before confirming the order, either cause a local inquiry to be held or give anyone who has objected an opportunity to be heard before someone appointed for that purpose. After considering the objections and the report of the person conducting the inquiry or hearing, the Secretary of State may confirm the order with or without modifications.

The order takes effect at a specified date, but this cannot be less than six months from the date of confirmation. It can be postponed if, before the order comes into effect, the authority passes a resolution postponing it. It must also publish a notice in respect of this in the press as described above. The order then comes into effect on the date specified in the resolution unless there is a further postponement. However, an order cannot be postponed for more than twelve months without the consent of the Secretary of State.

An order which varies an existing order by excluding specified buildings, classes of buildings or fireplaces from the scope of an order, may come into effect at any time on or after its confirmation, irrespective of the six-month period.

Any order made under the above procedure may be varied or revoked by a subsequent order properly made and confirmed. **s11/56, s10/68**

Under the above provisions a local authority has powers to declare a smoke control area, but the 1968 Act gives the Secretary of State powers to require authorities to declare smoke control areas. If, after consultation with the authority, the Secretary of State is satisfied the authority has either not exercised or not sufficiently exercised its powers, he may direct it to prepare and submit for approval proposals for bringing one or more smoke control orders into operation within a specified period of not less than six months.

The local authority may alter any proposals within the original period specified or within such longer period as the Secretary of State may allow. Any proposals may be approved by the Secretary of State, with or without modifications, or may be rejected. If the authority fails to submit proposals, or its proposals are rejected, the Secretary of State may make an order declaring the authority to be in default and directing it to use its powers in a specified manner and within a specified period. **s8/68**

Controls within a smoke control area

There are controls over air pollution in smoke control areas which a local authority can enforce, and which are not applicable outside them.

Smoke

It is an offence to emit smoke from the chimney of any building or from a chimney serving the furnace of any boiler or industrial plant which is attached to or temporarily fixed to or installed on land in a smoke control area.

In proceedings for a contravention of this provision, it will be a defence to prove that the emission of smoke occurred when an authorised fuel was being burnt. An authorised fuel is one declared to be so by the Secretary of State. Various regulations have been made for this purpose.

In addition, the Secretary of State has powers to make regulations exempting specified fireplaces from this provision if he is satisfied that they can be used to burn fuel other than authorised fuel without producing smoke or any substantial quantity of smoke, provided that any specified conditions are observed. Several sets of regulations have been made exempting fireplaces. The commonest condition is that the fireplace shall be installed, maintained and operated in accordance with the manufacturer's instructions so as to minimise the emission of smoke, and that only specified fuels are to be used. **s11/56**

Where alterations to existing appliances are necessary in order to comply with the requirements in a smoke control area, the local authority must, in certain circumstances, pay a proportion, and may pay the whole, of the costs involved in converting appliances in private dwellings. A local authority may also make contributions towards the expenses incurred in adapting appliances in churches,

139

church halls, chapels and similar premises, and in buildings occupied by organisations whose main objectives are concerned with charity, or other works of religion, education or social welfare. **ss12–15/56**

Unauthorised fuel

It is an offence:

(a) To acquire any solid fuel other than an authorised fuel for use in a smoke control area unless the building, fireplace, boiler or plant in which it is to be used is exempt from the controls.

(b) To sell by retail any solid fuel other than an authorised fuel for delivery to a building, or premises where there is plant or a boiler. It is a defence for a person charged with the offence to prove that he believed and had reasonable grounds for believing that the building was exempt or was not included in a class of buildings to which the order applied, or that the fuel was for use in a building, boiler or plant which was exempt or was not included in a class to which the smoke control order applied.

The maximum penalty on summary conviction for a contravention of this provision is a fine of £100. **s9/68**

Relaxation of controls

The Secretary of State, if he considers it expedient or necessary to do so, may by order suspend or relax the controls in s11 relating to a declared smoke control area. Before he does so, he must consult the local authority concerned unless there is a matter of urgency which makes it impracticable to do so.

Any such order may subsequently be varied or revoked by a further order. As soon as is practicable after the order has been made, the local authority must take steps to bring the effect of the order to the notice of persons affected. **s11(7)–(9)/56**

Smoke Nuisances

Smoke, other than:

(a) smoke emitted from a private dwelling;

(b) dark smoke emitted from a chimney of a building, from a chimney serving the furnace of a boiler or industrial plant attached to a building or temporarily fixed to or installed on any land, or from industrial or trade premises otherwise than from a chimney;

is to be a statutory nuisance for the purposes of the Public Health Act 1936, if it is a nuisance to the inhabitants of the neighbourhood.

It will be a defence in proceedings concerning the emission of smoke from a chimney to prove that the best practicable means had been used to prevent the nuisance.

If a local authority is satisfied that such a nuisance has occurred, and though ceased is likely to recur, it may, without serving an abatement notice, take proceedings by way of complaint to a magistrate's court. The court can make an order against any person by whose act, default or sufferance the nuisance arose, prohibit a recurrence of the nuisance and require him within a specified time to carry out any works necessary to prevent it. **s16/1956**

Relationship of the Clean Air Acts and the Alkali Act

The Clean Air Acts do not apply to any works subject to, or potentially subject to, the Alkali Act.

However, the Alkali Act applies to grit, dust and smoke from works subject to the Act in the same way as it does to noxious and offensive gases, ie, in the Alkali Act the classification of noxious or offensive gases is to be considered as including smoke, dust or grit, and the best practicable means must be used to prevent their emission into the atmosphere.

The enforcing authority in respect of such premises and emissions will be the Health and Safety Executive. Local authorities have no powers under the Clean Air Acts in respect of such premises, even where they are in a smoke control area.

However, on the application of the local authority, the Secretary of State may, by order, direct that in respect of any specified works subject to the Alkali Act the provisions of the Clean Air Acts shall be applicable, and the local authority will be able to enforce them.

While such an order is in force, in any proceedings for a contravention of the provisions concerning dark smoke, contravention of smoke control orders or smoke nuisances, it will be a defence to show that the best practicable means had been used to ensure compliance. **s11/68**

Exemptions for Investigation and Research

On the application of any person interested, a local authority may, if it thinks it expedient to do so for the purpose of enabling investigation and research relevant to the problems of air pollution to be carried out, exempt from all or any part of the Clean Air Acts, subject to conditions and for a specified period, a chimney, furnace, boiler, industrial plant, any premises, or the sale or acquisition of unauthorised fuel.

141

If the applicant is dissatisfied with the decision of the local authority, he may appeal to the Secretary of State who, if he thinks fit, may give any exemption which the authority might have given, or vary the terms of any exemption which had been granted. **s21/56**

Powers of the Court

If work must be carried out to a building so that it may be used without involving the contravention of some provision of the Acts and the occupier needs the consent of some other person interested in the building to carry such works out, and that consent cannot be obtained, he may apply to the County Court for an order to enable him to carry out those works.

If the occupier is of the opinion that the whole or any part of the cost should be borne by the owner of the building or some other interested person, he may apply to the County Court for an order directing the owner or other interested person to indemnify him either wholly or partly in respect of the cost of the works. In either case, the court may make such an order as appears to it to be just. **s28/56**

Duty to Notify of Offences

If an authorised officer of a local authority is of the opinion that an offence under the provisions relating to dark smoke or the emission of smoke in a smoke control area has been committed, or that a smoke nuisance exists, he must as soon as may be, unless he has reason to believe that a notice has already been given, notify the owner, occupier or person in charge of the premises. If this notification is not in writing, he must, within the period of four days following that on which he became aware of the offence, confirm the notice in writing. In proceedings under the provisions relating to dark smoke or smoke in a smoke control area, it will be a defence to prove that these requirements have not been complied with. If notice has not been given within the period of four days following the commission of the offence, the above requirements will be regarded as not having been complied with, unless the contrary is proved. **s30/56**

Disclosure of Information

It is an offence for any person to disclose any information relating to a trade secret used in any undertaking, furnished to him or obtained by him under or in connection with the execution of the Acts unless the disclosure is made:

(a) With the consent of the person who is carrying out that undertaking.
(b) In connection with the execution of the Act.
(c) For the purposes of any legal proceedings arising out of the Acts, or of any report of such proceedings. **s26/56**

Penalties

Except where specific provision is made, the maximum penalty for any offence under the Clean Air Acts is, on summary conviction, a fine of £400. However, where an offence is substantially a repetition or continuation of an earlier offence in respect of which where has been a conviction, the maximum penalty on summary conviction is a fine of £400, or £50 per day on which the offence continued or was repeated within three months following the conviction, whichever is the greater. **s27/56**

Metrication

Under the Control of Pollution Act 1974, the Secretary of State can make regulations to substitute amounts specified in metric units for amounts not so expressed. Such alterations must preserve the effect of the original provisions, except that minor alterations may be made to obtain convenient and suitable amounts in metric units. **CPA s103**

The Control of Pollution Act 1974

The Clean Air Acts were virtually unaffected by the 1974 Act. This Act, however, does give additional powers concerning air pollution in two broad areas: the control of the contents of oils, and research and publicity.

Regulations Governing the Contents of Oils

The Secretary of State is given power to make regulations concerning the contents of oils.

Motor fuel

The Secretary of State can make regulations to impose requirements as to the composition and contents of any fuel of a kind used in motor vehicles, in order to limit or reduce air pollution. The regulations may prevent or restrict the production, treatment, distribution, import, sale or use of any fuel which fails in any respect to comply with the requirements, and which is for use in the United Kingdom. Before such regulations are made, the Secretary of State must consult representatives of manufacturers and users of motor vehicle fuels, and such experts in the field as he considers appropriate.

The regulations can apply standards, tests and specifications laid down in documents not forming part of the regulations, and may authorise the Secretary of State to confer exemptions. In addition, in order to ensure that persons to whom fuel is supplied are given information as to the contents, the regulations may require information to be displayed at such places and in such a manner as may be specified.

Regulations have been made under this provision: the Motor Fuel (Sulphur Content of Gas Oil) Regulations 1976 (SI 1976 No 1989), which came into force on 29 December 1976.

These regulations apply to gas oil, which is defined as any liquid petroleum product used as a fuel in motor vehicles propelled by diesel engines of which less than 65 per cent by volume is distilled at 250°C, and more than 85 per cent at 350°C. The production, treatment, distribution, use, etc, of any gas oil is prohibited if the amount of sulphur exceeds 0·5 grammes per hundred grammes of oil during the period 29 December 1976 to 30 September 1980, and exceeds 0·3 grammes of sulphur per hundred grammes after 1 October 1980.

The regulations also contain certain exemptions.

The local weights and measures authorities are responsible for the enforcement of the regulations, using the provisions of the Trade Descriptions Act 1968. In brief, inspectors have power to make test purchases and to enter premises and inspect goods and documents. If tests are made on goods seized or purchased, notice of the tests must be given to the person from whom the goods were seized or purchased and, if practicable, he must be permitted to have tests carried out. Notice of an intended prosecution must be given to the Secretary of State who can stop prosecutions. **s75**

Oil fuel

Oil fuel is defined as any liquid petroleum product produced in a refinery. To limit or reduce air pollution, the Secretary of State may make regulations imposing limits on the sulphur content of oil fuel used in furnaces or engines, but he must first consult representatives of the producers and users of oil fuels, representatives of the manufacturers and users of plant and equipment in which oil fuel is used, and experts in the field of air pollution.

The regulations may prescribe the kinds of oil fuel and the kinds of furnaces and engines to which they apply, may apply tests, standards and specifications contained in documents not forming part of the regulations, may authorise the Secretary of State to confer exemptions, and may make different provisions for different areas. Regulations have been made under this power: the Oil Fuel (Sulphur Content of Gas Oil) Regulations 1976 (SI 1976 No 1988), which came into force on 29 December 1976.

The broad effect is as follows. These regulations apply to gas oil, defined as any liquid petroleum product produced in a refinery, of which less than 65 per cent by volume is distilled at 250°C and more than 85 per cent is distilled at 350°C. The maximum permitted amount of sulphur per hundred grammes of oil is 0·8 grammes between 29 September 1976 and 30 September 1980, and thereafter 0·5 grammes. No person shall use oil with more than the permitted maximum in any furnace or engine, other than a furnace or engine in a ship or power station or a diesel engine used to power a motor vehicle.

These regulations are enforced by local authorities except as regards furnaces in works to which the Alkali Act applies, when inspectors appointed by the Health and Safety Executive are responsible for enforcement. **s76**

Breach and penalties

Failure to comply with regulations made under these provisions is an offence. The maximum penalty which can be imposed is, on summary conviction, a fine of £400, unless the regulations themselves provide for a smaller maximum. A smaller penalty has been imposed under both sets of regulations. The maximum penalty for any contravention under the Oil Fuel Regulations is £50. Under the Motor Fuel Regulations there is a maximum penalty of £50 where the offence is committed in connection with a mobile crane, otherwise it is £400. On conviction on indictment, the maximum penalty can be an unlimited fine for a contravention of any regulations made under these provisions, but regulations themselves may exclude the possibility of trial on indictment. Both sets of regulations do, in fact, exclude trial on indictment for any breach. **s77**

Information about Air Pollution

Research and publicity

Under the Clean Air Act 1956, s25, a local authority can arrange lectures, exhibitions, etc, to publicise the problems of air pollution. The Control of Pollution Act 1974 gives local authorities greatly increased powers to obtain information and publicise the problem.

A local authority may undertake, or contribute towards the cost of, research and investigations relevant to the problem of air pollution and arrange for the publication of information. In particular, it may issue notices (see below), measure and record emissions and for that purpose enter premises either by agreement or under its powers of entry (see p 156), or make arrangements whereby occupiers measure and record emissions on its behalf. None of these powers can be used in respect of a private dwelling.

Before exercising any of these powers, the local authority must consult persons engaged in trade or business in the area or their representatives, experts on the problem of air pollution, and those interested in the amenities of the locality about the way in which the local authority should exercise its powers and about the manner and extent of publication of the results. These consultations must take place at least twice in each financial year.

A local authority is authorised to investigate works subject to the Alkali Act only by the issuing of a notice, or by investigation and research without entering the premises. s79

Power of entry

A local authority may use its powers of entry under s91 for the purpose of measuring and recording emissions only if it has given the occupier of the premises concerned a notice specifying the kinds of emission in question and the steps it proposes to take to measure them. The authority may not enter the premises until twenty-one days after the date when the notice was issued.

The notice must contain a statement that the authority intends to use its powers of entry for this purpose unless the occupier requests the authority to serve a notice under s80 (see below). If such a request is made, then the procedure relating to notices must be followed. Any information published as a result of the exercise of the power of entry or as a result of entry by agreement must be presented in such a way that no information relating to a trade secret is disclosed, except with the consent of the person authorised to disclose it or with the consent of the Secretary of State. Breach of this duty is actionable. **s79 (3), (5), (6)**

Notices requiring information

The following provisions do not apply to premises used as a private dwelling. If the notice relates to premises subject to the Alkali Act, the person on whom the notice is served need supply no information which an inspector appointed to enforce that Act certifies need not be supplied under that Act.

A local authority may serve a notice on the occupier of premises in its area requiring him to furnish, whether by periodical returns or otherwise, such information as may be specified in the notice concerning the emission of pollutants and other matters into the atmosphere. A person on whom this notice is served must comply with its terms within six weeks or such longer period as the local authority may allow. A notice served under this provision cannot require returns at intervals of less than three months, and no notice can cover a period exceeding twelve months.

Failure to comply with the terms of a notice without reasonable excuse is an offence, as is knowingly or recklessly to make a statement in a return which is false in a material particular.

The maximum penalty is, on summary conviction, a fine of £400. Following a conviction, a local authority may use its power of entry to obtain the information, and the provision which stops this power being exercisable by a request for a notice is not applicable. **s80**

Appeals against notices

A person served with a notice, or any other person interested in the premises to which the notice relates, may appeal to the Secretary of State on the following grounds:

(a) That the giving of the information to the local authority or the disclosure of all or part of it to the public would prejudice to an unreasonable degree some private interest by disclosing information about a trade secret, or would be contrary to the public interest.

(b) That the information required is not immediately available, and cannot be readily obtained or collected without incurring undue expenditure.

If the Secretary of State allows the appeal, he may direct the local authority to withdraw or modify the notice, or take such steps as may be specified to ensure that prejudicial information is not disclosed to the public.

147

The Secretary of State is empowered to make regulations for the detailed procedure to be followed on appeal. This power has been exercised: the Control of Atmospheric Pollution (Appeals) Regulations 1977 (SI 1977 No 17) came into force on 7 February 1977.

The notice of appeal must be in writing, to the Secretary of State, during the period allowed for compliance with the notice. It must be in duplicate, must specify on which of the grounds the appeal is made, the facts and the reasons for it. A copy of the notice and any other relevant documents must also be supplied.

Where the Secretary of State is satisfied that the disclosure of any information would be prejudicial to an unreasonable degree to a private interest by disclosing information relating to a trade secret, or would be contrary to the public interest, he shall withhold from the local authority any statement given by the appellant specifying the facts and reasons for the appeal, and any other document containing the information. Subject to this, he must send the local authority a copy of the notice of appeal and any other document.

The Secretary of State may require the appellant or the local authority to submit a further statement in respect of any of the matters to which the appeal relates, and he may decide the appeal if satisfied that he is sufficiently informed. In any other case, unless he causes a local inquiry to be held, he must, if either party so wishes, give each of them an opportunity to be heard before a person appointed for that purpose. **s81**

Exemptions

The provisions relating to notices apply to Crown premises unless regulations provide otherwise, although in respect of these premises a local authority is not permitted to use its powers of entry and inspection, or powers to require information.

Certain premises have been exempted by the Control of Atmospheric Pollution (Exempted Premises) Regulations 1977 (SI 1977 No 18). These broadly comprise the category of premises relating to defence and national security.

Regulations covering research and publicity

After consulting representatives of local authorities and industry, and experts in the problems of air pollution, the Secretary of State must make regulations to prescribe the manner in which and the methods by which local authorities are to perform their functions in connection with research and publicity.

These regulations may provide for matters such as the kinds of emissions to which notices may relate, the sort of information notices may require, the service of notices, the keeping of a register of information, the circumstances in which a local authority may enter into agreements with the occupiers of premises whereby they will make recordings on behalf of the authority, and the kinds of apparatus for measuring air pollution which a local authority may provide and use.

Regulations have been made under this provision. The Control of Atmospheric Pollution (Research and Publicity) Regulations 1977 (SI 1977 No 19) came into force on 7 February 1977.

A notice may relate to the emission of pollutants and other substances from any outlet used for the discharge from premises to the atmosphere of:

(a) Sulphur dioxide or particulate matter derived from any combustion process where the material being heated does not contribute to the emission.

(b) Any gas or particulate matter derived from any combustion process where the material being heated contributes to the emission.

(c) Any gas or particulate matter derived from any non-combustion process or other similar industrial activity.

The notice must specify the premises to which it relates, and may require information such as the aggregate duration of discharges, the temperature, the velocity and volume of emissions, the height above ground level at which it is made, and the average concentration and the aggregate quantities during the specified period.

A notice may only require information in respect of an earlier discharge if the information is held by the occupier, or readily available to him.

A local authority must keep a register of all the information obtained by notices and by measurement and recording of emissions, and from arrangements whereby occupiers record emissions. If as the result of an appeal the Secretary of State has directed that information shall not be disclosed, that fact must be recorded. The register must also contain a note of all appeals which were not dismissed by the Secretary of State, stating date, grounds for appeal and result. It must be adequately indexed so that information relating to particular premises can be found. It must be kept open for public inspection at all reasonable times, and the public must be able, on payment of a reasonable charge, to obtain copies of the entries. **s82**

Provision of information to the Secretary of State

The Secretary of State, after consultations with the local authority concerned, may direct it to make specified arrangements for the provision, installation, operation and maintenance of apparatus for measuring and recording air pollution, and for transmission of the information to him. Where such apparatus is provided, the Secretary of State must defray the whole of the capital expenditure involved. **s83**

Enforcement

To enforce the Clean Air Acts, local authorities have the powers conferred by the Public Health Act 1936. To enforce the applicable provisions of the Control of Pollution Act they may exercise the powers contained in that Act (see p 151).

CHAPTER SIX

ENFORCEMENT

Various aspects of enforcement have been dealt with in earlier chapters; this chapter is concerned with those powers which apply under more than one heading.

Two main sets of provisions need to be examined, those under the Public Health Act 1936 and those under the Control of Pollution Act 1974.

The Public Health Act 1936

Local authorities can exercise their powers under this Act to enforce the Public Health Act 1936, the Clean Air Acts 1956 and 1968 (and also the Deposit of Poisonous Waste Act 1972). These powers are also available to water authorities in the exercise of their functions under the legislation relating to trade effluents. In addition to the following, the Act also deals with various procedural matters such as the service of notices and the authentification of documents.

Power of Entry

Any authorised officer of a local authority and, for this purpose only, an officer of a water authority when enforcing the trade effluent legislation, shall, on the production if requested of a duly authenticated document showing his authority, have a right to enter any premises at all reasonable hours for the following purposes:

PROBLEM	SUBSTANTIVE PROVISIONS	ENFORCING/LICENSING AUTHORITY	ENFORCEMENT POWERS
Statutory nuisances	Public Health Act 1936	Local Authority	Public Health Act 1936
Discharge of liquid effluent to rivers, tidal waters or underground	Control of Pollution Act 1974[1]	Water Authority	Control of Pollution Act 1974
Discharge of liquid effluent to sewers	Public Health (Drainage of Trade Premises) Act 1937[2]	Water Authority	Public Health Act 1936
Disposal of waste on land	Control of Pollution Act 1974[3]	Disposal Authority	Control of Pollution Act 1974
Noise	Control of Pollution Act 1974[4]	Local Authority	Control of Pollution Act 1974
Air pollution	(1) Alkali etc. Works Regulation Act 1906[5]	Health and Safety Executive	Health and Safety at Work Act 1974
	(2) Clean Air Acts 1956, 1968	Local Authority	Public Health Act 1936
	(3) Control of Pollution Act 1974	Local Authority	Control of Pollution Act 1974
Dumping of waste at sea	Dumping at Sea Act 1974	Minister of Agriculture, Fisheries and Food	Dumping at Sea Act 1974
Town and country planning	Town and Country Planning Act 1971	Local Planning Authority	Town and Country Planning Act 1971

[1]This will eventually replace the Rivers (Prevention of Pollution) Acts 1951 and 1961, the Clean Rivers (Estuaries and Tidal Waters) Act 1960, and part of the Water Resources Act 1963; until it does so, water authorities are responsible for enforcing these Acts.

[2]As amended by the Public Health Act 1961 and the Control of Pollution Act 1974.

[3]This Act replaces the Deposit of Poisonous Waste Act 1972.

[4]This Act replaces the Noise Abatement Act 1960.

[5]Eventually this Act will be replaced by regulations made under the Health and Safety at Work Act 1974. This Act and any regulations which may be made only apply to premises of a specified description.

(a) To ascertain whether there is or has been on or in connection with the premises a contravention of any provision of any Act for which the authority is responsible for enforcement.

(b) To ascertain whether or not circumstances exist to authorise or require the authority to take any action or execute any works.

(c) To take any action or execute any works authorised to be taken or exercised by any Act.

(d) Generally for the purpose of the exercise by the authority of its functions.

This power may not be exercised as of right in connection with premises which are not a factory, workshop or workplace, unless at least twenty-four hours' notice of the intended entry has been given to the occupier. It may not be exercised at all in respect of a private dwelling in connection with the Clean Air Acts except under s12(2) of the 1956 Act where work is necessary to avoid the emission of smoke in a smoke control area.

Where a Justice of the Peace is satisfied that admission has been refused or that such a refusal is apprehended, or that the premises are unoccupied or that the owner is temporarily absent, or that the case is urgent, or that an application for admission would defeat the purpose of entry, and that there are reasonable grounds for entry, he may, by warrant, authorise entry to the premises, by force if necessary.

A warrant may be issued only if the Justice of the Peace is satisfied that either notice of the intention to apply for it has been given, or that the giving of such notice is either impossible or inadvisable.

An authorised officer entering premises under warrant may take with him such other persons as may be necessary, and on leaving unoccupied premises must leave them as secure against trespassers as he found them. **s287**

A person who obstructs any person acting in the execution of the Acts or any orders or warrants will be liable to a fine not exceeding £10 for a first offence, or £20 for a second or subsequent offence. **s288**

Disclosure of Information

Any person who gains admission to a factory, workshop or work-place either under the power of entry or by warrant, and discloses to any person any information he gains relating to a manufacturing process or trade secret, unless the disclosure was made in the course of his duty, shall be guilty of an offence and be liable to a maximum penalty of a fine of £100 or three months' imprisonment. **s287(5)**

Power to Require an Occupier to Permit Works

If a magistrate's court is satisfied that the occupier of premises is preventing the owner from executing any works which, by or under the Act, he is required to execute, the court may order the occupier to permit them. **s289**

Notices Requiring Works

Any notice requiring works to be carried out must indicate their nature and specify a time limit during which they must be done. A person served with such a notice may appeal to a magistrate's court on any of the following grounds:

(a) That the notice or a requirement is not justified by the terms of the relevant section.
(b) That there has been some informality, defect or error in or in connection with the notice. If the court is satisfied that this was not material, it must dismiss the appeal.
(c) That the authority has unreasonably refused to approve the execution of alternative works, or that the works are otherwise unreasonable in character or extent, or are unnecessary.
(d) That the time within which the works must be carried out is not reasonably sufficient for the purpose.
(e) That the notice might lawfully have been served on the occupier of the premises in question instead of the owner, or on the owner instead of the occupier, and that it would have been equitable for it to have been so served.
(f) Where the work is for the common benefit of the premises and other premises, that some other person being the owner or occupier of the other premises should contribute towards the cost of the works.

Where the grounds of the appeal is (e) or (f), the appellant must serve a copy of the notice of appeal on the other person referred to and, in the case of any appeal, may serve a copy on any person interested in the premises.

The court may make such an order as it thinks fit concerning the person by whom the works are to be carried out, the contribution to be made by any other person towards their cost, or the proportion in which expenses are to be recoverable from various persons by the local authority. In making such an order the court must have regard to the terms and conditions of any tenancy, the nature of the works required and the degree of benefit to be derived by the various persons.

Unless the recipient of the notice appeals, he must comply with the notice within the period specified. Failure to do so is an offence with a maximum penalty of £50 and £2 per day on which the offence continues after conviction. In addition, the local authority may carry out the works and recover from the person in default any reasonable costs. In any proceedings for the recovery of the expenses, the person in default cannot raise any question which he could have raised in an appeal against the notice. **s290**

Such expenses owing to the authority may be recovered from the person who is the owner of the premises at the time the works are completed. If, however, he has ceased to be the owner before the demand for payment is served, the authority may recover the amount either from him or from the new owner. From the date of service of the demand for payment, the expenses and interest are a charge on the property. **s291**

Legal Proceedings

The procedure for an appeal or determination by a magistrate's court is to be by way of complaint for an order. Proceedings must be started within twenty-one days from the date on which the notice was served on the appellant. In any case where such a right of appeal exists, the notice must contain a statement on the right of appeal, and the time limit. **s300**

Without the consent of the Attorney General, proceedings under the Act may not be instituted by any person other than an aggrieved party or a local authority responsible for enforcing the Act. **s298**

Local Inquiries

The Secretary of State may cause a local inquiry to be held in cases where he has power under the Act to give consents, confirmations, etc, or to make any order or determine any difference, or to take any action under the Act or in any case where he deems it advisable that a public inquiry should be held concerning any matter relating to public health in any place. **s318**

Control of Pollution Act 1974

The Act gives powers to relevant authorities and their authorised officers to carry out their functions under the Act. These relevant authorities are defined as the Secretary of State, a water authority, a county council, a district council, a London borough council, the Common Council of the City of London, the Sub-Treasurer of the Inner Temple and the Under Treasurer of the Middle Temple. In particular, the various powers conferred by the Act can be exercised in connection with the problems of the disposal of waste on land, water pollution, noise, and certain provisions concerning air pollution.

Entry and Inspection

A person authorised by a relevant authority may at any reasonable time enter upon any land or vessel:

(a) To perform any function conferred on that person or authority by the Act.
(b) To determine whether and, if so, how such a function should be performed.
(c) To determine whether the provisions of the Act or any instrument made under it are being complied with.
(d) To carry out such inspections, measurements and tests on the land or vessel, or any articles on the land or vessel, and to take away such samples as are considered appropriate.

If a Justice of the Peace is satisfied that admission has been refused, a refusal is apprehended, the land or vessel is unoccupied, the occupier is temporarily absent, there is an emergency, or that to request entry would defeat the purpose, and that there are reasonable grounds for requiring entry, he may issue a warrant authorising entry.

A Justice of the Peace must not issue a warrant unless he is satisfied as to one of the following:

(1) That admission has been sought after not less than seven days' notice has been served on the occupier.
(2) That admission has been sought in an emergency and has been refused.
(3) That the land or vessel is unoccupied.
(4) That an application for admission would defeat the purpose.

A person authorised to enter may take with him such other persons and equipment as may be necessary, and he must, if requested, produce evidence of his authority.

Admission to land or a vessel used for residential purposes and admission onto any land or vessel with heavy equipment shall not be demanded as of right, unless at least seven days' notice of the intended entry has been given, except where there is an emergency or where the land or vessel is unoccupied.

If a person enters land or a vessel which is unoccupied or where the owner is temporarily absent, he must leave it as secure against trespassers as he found it. A relevant authority must compensate any person who has sustained damage as the result of the exercise of these powers by an authorised person, or as the result of a failure to leave premises secure, unless the damage was caused by the fault of the person who sustained it. If there is a dispute as to the entitlement to compensation, the matter is to be settled by arbitration.

It is an offence wilfully to obstruct any person in the exercise of these powers, punishable on summary conviction with a maximum fine of £100.

For the above provisions an emergency is defined as any case where the person requiring entry has reasonable cause to believe that circumstances exist which are likely to endanger life or health, and that immediate entry is necessary to verify the existence of the circumstances, to ascertain their cause or to effect a remedy.

A disposal authority is not entitled to exercise these powers in connection with waste which is not controlled waste. **ss91, 92**

Power to Require Information

A relevant authority may serve on any person a notice requiring him to furnish, within a specified time and in a specified form, any specified information which it considers necessary for the purpose of any function conferred on it by the Act. Regulations may be made to restrict the information which may be required and to determine the form in which it may be required.

Failure to comply with such a notice without reasonable excuse, or knowingly or recklessly to make a statement which is false in a material particular, is an offence punishable on summary conviction with a maximum fine of £400. **s93**

In addition to this general power, authorities have other specific powers relating, for example, to waste other than controlled waste (s19) and to the obtaining of information about air pollution.

Disclosure of Information

If information relating to any trade secret used in carrying on an undertaking has been given to a person or has been obtained by him by virtue of the Act, the disclosure of it will be an offence with a maximum penalty on summary conviction of a fine of £400.

Disclosure will not be an offence if:

(a) It is made in the course of his duty.
(b) It is made in pursuance of s79(1)(b), that is, publicity of information relating to air pollution.
(c) It is made with the consent in writing of the person authorised to disclose it.
(d) The information is of a kind which regulations prescribe may be disclosed and, if they prescribe persons to whom it may be disclosed, it is disclosed to a person of that description. **s94**

Legal Proceedings

An appeal against a decision of the magistrate's court, other than in criminal proceedings, lies to the Crown Court at the instance of any party to it.

Where there is an appeal to the Crown Court against a decision dismissing an appeal against a notice, and the notice was suspended pending the determination of the appeal by the magistrate's court, the effect of the notice will be suspended pending the determination of the appeal by the Crown Court.

Where there is a right of appeal against a decision of any relevant authority, any document notifying the authority's decision must contain a statement of the right of appeal and must specify the time within which it must be brought.

Where an offence committed by a body corporate is proved to have been committed with the consent or connivance of, or to have been attributable to the neglect of, any director, manager, secretary or other similar officer, then he, as well as the body corporate, will be guilty of the offence and will be liable to be proceeded against and punished.

Where the commission by any person of an offence is due to the act or default of any other person, then that other person will be guilty of the offence and may be charged with and convicted of it, whether or not proceedings are taken against any other person. **ss85,87**

Local Inquiries

Where he considers it appropriate the Secretary of State may cause a local inquiry to be held either in connection with a provision of the Act or with a view to preventing or dealing with pollution or noise at any place. **s96**

Local Government (Miscellaneous Provisions) Act 1976

Power to Obtain Information about Land

A local authority may exercise the following powers with a view to performing a function conferred on it by any enactment. This provision is applicable only to local authorities.

To obtain information relating to any land, the authority may serve a notice on one or more persons who are occupiers of the land, anyone who has an interest in land either as a freeholder, lessee or mortgagee, or who directly or indirectly receives rent, or any person who is authorised to manage the land or arrange for its letting.

The notice must specify the land, the function and the enactment and must require the recipient to furnish, within a specified period of not less than fourteen days from the date of service, information concerning the nature of his interest, the name and address of each person he believes to be in occupation of the land, and the name and address of each person he believes to be included in the category of persons on whom the notice may be served.

Failure to comply with such a notice, or knowingly or recklessly to make a statement which is false in a material particular, is an offence punishable on summary conviction with a maximum fine of £400. **s16**

CHAPTER SEVEN

OTHER RELEVANT LEGISLATION

The Dumping at Sea Act 1974

The Control of Pollution Act 1974, together with other legislation, deals with the problems of the disposal of waste on land and the pollution of inland and coastal waters.

The dumping of waste at sea is subject to control under the Dumping at Sea Act 1974, and the pattern of the legislation is similar. In broad terms, an activity is made a criminal offence unless it is carried on under the authority of, and in accordance with, the terms of a licence issued by a licensing authority. The Act implements two international conventions for the prevention of marine pollution by the dumping of waste at sea.

Offences

It is an offence:
(a) To dump substances or articles in UK waters, ie, within UK territorial waters.
(b) To dump substances or articles in the sea outside UK waters from a British ship, aircraft, hovercraft or marine structure.
(c) To load substances or articles onto a ship, aircraft, hovercraft or marine structure in the UK or in UK waters for dumping at sea, whether in UK waters or not.
(d) To cause or permit any dumping or loading as mentioned in (a), (b) and (c).

160

For the purpose of the Act, an article or substance is dumped if it is permanently deposited in the sea from a ship, aircraft, hovercraft or marine structure, or from a structure on land constructed or adapted for the purpose of depositing solids in the sea.

A discharge incidental to the normal operation of a ship, etc, is not dumping unless the ship, etc, is constructed for the disposal of waste or spoil, and the discharge takes place as part of those operations.

Also, a deposit made by or with the consent of a harbour or lighthouse authority to provide moorings or aids to navigation does not constitute dumping, nor does a deposit made by or on behalf of a harbour authority in the execution of maintenance works in a harbour, if the deposit is made on the site of the works. **s1(1)–(5)**

Defences

There are defences to this apparently blanket prohibition:

(a) That the dumping was authorised by and in accordance with the terms of a licence issued by the relevant licensing authority.

(b) Where the dumping was from a British ship, aircraft or hovercraft, that the substance was loaded in a foreign country which was a party to the conventions, and that the dumping was authorised by a licence given by a responsible authority in that state.

(c) That the substance or article was dumped to secure the safety of the ship, etc, or to save life, and that within a reasonable time the Minister was informed of that fact, of the locality, of the circumstances of the dumping and of the nature and quantity of substances dumped, unless the court is satisfied that the dumping was not necessary for any of the above purposes and was not a reasonable step to take.

(d) That the person charged acted on instructions given to him by his employer, or that he acted in reliance on information given by others and had no reason to suspect that the information was false and misleading, provided that in either case he took all reasonable steps to ensure that no offence was committed. **s1(7)–(9)**

Penalties

The maximum penalties for a contravention of the above provisions are, on summary conviction, a fine of £400 or six months' imprisonment, or both, and on conviction on indictment, five years' imprisonment, an unlimited fine, or both. **s1(6)**

Licences

The most important defence to a charge of unauthorised dumping is that it was done with the authority of and in accordance with the terms of a licence issued by the relevant authority.

Licensing authorities are:

(a) In relation to substances or articles loaded in England and Wales or in UK waters adjacent to England and Wales, or loaded outside the UK and outside UK waters, the Minister of Agriculture, Fisheries and Food.
(b) In relation to substances loaded in Scotland or in UK waters adjacent to Scotland, the Secretary of State for Scotland.
(c) In relation to substances loaded in Northern Ireland or in UK waters adjacent to Northern Ireland, the Department of the Environment for Northern Ireland. **s12**

Applications

In deciding whether to grant a licence, the licensing authority must take into consideration the need to protect the sea and marine life from the adverse effects of substances it is proposed to dump. Any conditions the authority considers necessary to achieve such protection must be included in the licence.

When the authority is considering whether to grant the licence and possible conditions to be attached, the applicant may be required to supply information about, and to permit the examination and sampling of, the articles or substances involved or similar substances or articles, and to furnish information about the methods of dumping.

With the consent of the Treasury, the authority may require an applicant to pay a fee in respect of the application, and to contribute towards the costs of any tests necessary in deciding whether to grant a licence and, in particular, to cover the costs of monitoring in order to ascertain the effect the dumping has had or might have on sea and marine life.

The licence must:

(a) Specify the person to whom it is granted.
(b) State whether it is to remain in force until it is revoked or is to expire at a specified time.

(c) Specify the quantity and description of the substances or articles to which it relates.

Different provisions in the licence may be made for different substances or articles. **s2(1), (4)–(7)**

Variation and revocation

A licensing authority may vary or revoke a licence if it appears that this is necessary because of a change of circumstances relating to the marine environment or marine life, including a change in scientific knowledge.

A licensing authority may also revoke a licence if it appears that the holder is in breach of any condition contained in it. Conviction for an offence under the Act is not necessary for such revocation. **s2(2), (3)**

Transfer

An authority may transfer a licence from the holder to some other person on the application of the holder or the other person, but it may impose additional conditions on transferring the licence. **s2(8)**

False statements

Knowingly or recklessly to make a false statement in connection with the granting or transfer of a licence, or in connection with the carrying out of some obligation imposed by the licence, eg, furnishing returns, is an offence carrying a maximum penalty on summary conviction of £400. **s2(9)**

Transitional provisions

The provisions of the Act supersede a previous voluntary system. Where there was in force an authorisation in writing from a licensing authority when the Act was passed, on 27 June 1974, provided that the terms are observed the dumping may continue until the authorisation expires or is revoked, ie, the authorisation has effect as if it were a licence issued under the Act. **s2(10)**

Representations

Where a licensing authority decides to refuse an application for a licence, to include a condition in the grant or transfer of a licence, to require payments for tests, etc, or to vary or revoke a licence, it must, when informing the applicant or the licence holder, notify him of the reasons for the decision and of his right to make representations. Where the decision is to vary or revoke a licence, there must also be a statement that written representations must be received within twenty-eight days from the receipt of the notification.

If representations are made they must be considered by a committee chosen from the members of a panel of suitably qualified people drawn up by the licensing authority for this purpose. The chairman of the committee must serve on the person who made the representations a notice requiring him to state whether he wants to appear and speak to the committee. Not earlier than the date of this notice, this person must also be informed of the date, place and time when the committee will consider his case. This must be not less than twenty-one days later, unless there is agreement on a shorter period. At the meeting the committee must consider the written and any oral representation made either by the appellant or by someone speaking on his behalf.

The authority cannot finally decide the matter until it has received and considered the committee's report of its findings and recommendations. The person concerned must be informed of the authority's decision and be given a copy of the report. Where the final result is a confirmation of the authority's original decision, no costs are payable. Subject to this, the authority can make such payment as it considers appropriate in connection with any costs or expenses incurred by the applicant in making representations and the consideration of them. **s3**

Publicity

A licensing authority must keep a register of notifiable particulars of dumping licensed by it. This register must be kept open for public inspection, and the public must be able to obtain copies of the information in it. The particulars which must be included are those the Government is obliged to give to the international organisations set up under the conventions, which cover matters such as the scale and distribution of dumping and the types of article and substance dumped. **s4**

Enforcement

Each licensing authority may appoint enforcement officers who may either be appointed specifically to enforce this Act or be officers of the authority appointed to perform these duties, subject to any limitations of their appointment.

An enforcement officer has power to enter land, buildings, vehicles, aircraft and hovercraft in the UK, ships in port in the UK, and British ships, aircraft, hovercraft and marine structures wherever they may be, if he has reasonable cause to believe that substances or articles for dumping in the sea are or have been present.

This power of entry does not extend to a private dwelling not used for the purposes of a trade or business. An officer may take with him persons or equipment to enable him to carry out his functions. He is empowered to stop a vehicle, ship, aircraft or hovercraft, and can require anything to be done to facilitate the boarding of it. He may also require the captain, master or any other person in control to attend and assist in inquiries.

The powers available to an officer are:

(a) To open any container, and examine and take samples of any substances or articles.
(b) To examine any equipment, and require any person in charge of it to do anything the inspector considers necessary to facilitate the examination.
(c) To require any person to produce any licence, records or other documents relating to the dumping of articles or substances in the sea which are in his custody or control.
(d) To compel any person on board a ship, aircraft, hovercraft or marine structure to produce any records or other documents which relate to it and which are in his custody or control.
(e) To take copies of any documents produced as a result of the exercise of his powers.

On entering or boarding any place or thing liable to inspection, an inspector must produce his certificate of authority. **s5**

There is provision in the Act for reciprocal enforcement arrangements to be concluded between the UK and other states which are parties to the Conventions. Under these, British enforcement officers would be able to exercise their powers outside UK waters in respect of ships or hovercraft of those foreign states; in return, enforcement officers of those foreign states would be able to exercise their powers in respect of British ships outside UK waters. **s6**

Neither a British nor a foreign enforcement officer will be liable in any criminal proceedings for anything done in the purported exercise of powers given under the Act if the court is satisfied that he acted in good faith and that there were reasonable grounds for his doing what he did. **s7(1)**

Any person who, without reasonable excuse, fails to comply with a requirement imposed by an enforcement officer or fails to answer a question asked by him, or who prevents or attempts to prevent another person from complying or answering, or who assaults or obstructs an officer in the exercise of his powers under the Act, will be guilty of an offence.

The maximum penalty for one of these offences is, on summary conviction for a first offence, a fine of £200, and for a second or subsequent offence, a fine of £400. **s7(2)**

Legal Proceedings

In any civil or criminal proceedings, a written statement made by an enforcement officer on matters ascertained in the exercise of his powers will be admissible in evidence to the same extent as oral evidence to the same effect. **s8**

Where an offence has been committed by a body corporate and it is proved that it was committed with the consent or connivance of, or was attributable to the neglect of, any director, manager, secretary or other officer, then he, as well as the body corporate, will be guilty of an offence and liable to be proceeded against and punished. **s9**

The restrictions imposed under the Act are in addition to any restriction imposed by any other Act, and neither affect nor are affected by that other enactment.

Nothing in the Act is to be treated as conferring a right of action in civil proceedings in respect of a contravention, or to limit in any way any civil or criminal action or remedy which exists apart from the Act. However, where an act is an offence under this Act, and also under some other Act or at common law, then only one set of proceedings can be taken in respect of it, and a conviction under one is a bar to proceedings under the other, thus ensuring that there cannot be two prosecutions for the same act or omission. **s13**

Oil Pollution at Sea: The Prevention of Oil Pollution Act 1971

This Act makes the discharge of oil into waters a criminal offence, and contains other provisions to deal with this problem.

166

Offences

It is an offence:

(a) To discharge any crude oil, fuel oil, lubricating oil, heavy diesel oil as defined, and any other oil specified in regulations, into the sea outside UK waters from a ship registered in the UK. No other oil has yet been specified. Certain exceptions from this provision have been made in the Oil in Navigable Waters (Exceptions) Regulations 1972 (SI 1972 No 1928).

Heavy diesel oil is defined in the Oil in Navigable Waters (Heavy Diesel Oil) Regulations 1967 (SI 1967 No 710) as marine diesel oil other than those distillates of which more than half the volume distils at a temperature not exceeding 340°C. The owner or master of the ship or both, may be convicted of an offence under this section. **s1**

(b) To discharge any oil or any mixture containing oil into the sea within UK territorial waters, and all other waters within those limits which are navigable by seagoing ships, ie, this section also applies to some inland waters. The following may be guilty of an offence:

  (i) Where the discharge is from a vessel, the owner or master of the vessel, or both, unless the discharge took place in the course of a transfer of the oil from the vessel to another vessel, or to a place on land, and he can prove that the discharge was caused by the act or omission of any person in charge of any apparatus on that other vessel or place. In this case the owner or master, or both, of that other vessel, or the occupier of the place will be guilty.

  (ii) If the discharge was from a place on land, then the occupier of that place will be liable unless he can prove that the discharge was caused by a person who was in that place without his permission, in which case that other person will be guilty.

  (iii) If the discharge takes place otherwise than is mentioned above, and is the result of the exploration of the sea bed or subsoil or the exploitation of their natural resources, then the person carrying on the operations will be liable. **s2**

(c) To discharge any oil or mixture containing oil into any part of the sea from a pipeline or otherwise than from a ship as the result of the exploration of the sea bed or subsoil or the exploitation of their natural resources in a designated area, that is, an area designated by an Order under the Continental Shelf

Act 1964. The owner of the pipeline or the person carrying on the operations will be guilty of an offence unless, in the latter case, he can prove that the discharge was from a place in his occupation and that it was due to the act of a person who was there without his permission. **s3**

Defences

Owner or master of a vessel

Where the owner or master of a vessel is charged under s1 or s2, it will be a defence to prove that the oil or mixture was discharged to secure the safety of any vessel, to prevent damage to any vessel or cargo, or to save life, unless the court is satisfied that the discharge was not necessary for that purpose or was not a reasonable step to take in the circumstances.

It will also be a defence to prove that the discharge occurred as a result of damage to the vessel and that as soon as was practicable all reasonable steps were taken to prevent the escape of the oil or mixture or, if it could not be prevented, that all steps were taken to stop or reduce the escape.

It will also be a defence to prove that the discharge occurred as the result of a leakage, that neither the leakage nor any delay in discovering it was due to a failure to take reasonable care and that as soon as was practicable all reasonable steps were taken to stop or reduce the discharge. **s5**

Other persons

Where a person is charged under s2 or s3 above as the occupier of any place, the owner of a pipeline, or a person carrying on operations, it will be a defence to prove that neither the escape nor any delay in discovering it was due to any failure to take reasonable care and that as soon as was practicable all reasonable steps were taken to stop or reduce the discharge.

Where someone is charged under s2 above in respect of the discharge of an oil mixture from land, it will be a defence to prove that the oil was contained in an effluent produced by operations for refining the oil, that it was not reasonably practicable to dispose of the effluent otherwise than by discharging it into the waters and that all reasonable steps were taken to eliminate the oil from the effluent.

This defence is not applicable if, at the time of the discharge, the surface of the waters or land adjacent to them was fouled by oil, unless the court is satisfied that the fouling was not caused or contributed to by oil contained in effluent discharged at or before that time at that place. **s6**

Miscellaneous

Where oil or a mixture containing oil is discharged as a result of the exercise of statutory powers for the removal of wrecks, the prevention of an obstruction or danger to navigation, or the disposal of sunk, stranded or abandoned vessels, no offence will be committed under s2 unless it is shown that there was a failure to take all reasonable steps to prevent, stop or reduce the discharge. **s7**

Penalties

The maximum penalties which can be imposed for an offence under any of the above are, on summary conviction, a fine of £50000, and on conviction on indictment, an unlimited fine.

Miscellaneous Provisions

Discharges in harbours

A harbour authority may appoint a place where the ballast water of vessels in which petroleum spirit has been carried may be discharged into the waters of the harbour at such times and subject to such conditions as the authority may determine.

Where such a place has been appointed, a discharge will not be an offence under s2 if made at that place, and at the time, and in accordance with the specified conditions, and the ballast water contains no oil other than petroleum spirit. **s8**

Facilities

A harbour authority may provide oil reception facilities to enable vessels using the harbour to discharge or deposit oil residues. The authority may make reasonable charges for the use of such facilities and may impose conditions regulating their use. These facilities are to be open to all vessels using the harbour but the authority need not make them available for tankers or for the reception of oil residues to enable a vessel to be repaired.

A harbour authority need not permit the reception of untreated ballast water into the facilities, ie, ballast water containing oil which has not been treated so as to separate the oil from the water.

If after consultation with a harbour authority and an organisation representing owners of ships registered in the UK the Secretary of State is satisfied that existing facilities in a harbour are inadequate, or that they do not exist but are necessary, he may direct the authority to provide or arrange for the provision of oil reception facilities.

Failure to comply with such a direction is a criminal offence for which a harbour authority will be liable to a maximum penalty on summary conviction of a fine of £10 per day on which the offence continues. **s9**

Equipment

The Secretary of State has power to make regulations requiring ships registered in the UK to be fitted with equipment and to comply with other specified requirements to prevent or reduce discharges of oil and mixtures containing oil into the sea.

Two sets of regulations have been made. The Oil in Navigable Waters (Ships' Equipment) (No 1) Regulations 1956 (SI 1956 No 1423) apply to ships which use oil as a fuel for engines or boilers. Such ships must be fitted so as to prevent oil fuel leaking from the bilges unless the contents of the bilges are subjected to an effective means of separating the oil from them before they are discharged into the sea. The Oil in Navigable Waters (Ships' Equipment) Regulations 1957 (SI 1957 No 1424) apply to ships which have a gross tonnage of 80 tons or more, and are not tankers, and which use their bunker fuel tanks for ballast water. Such ships must be fitted with an oily water separator to prevent or reduce discharges of oil and mixtures containing oil into the sea.

If such regulations are contravened, the owner, or master, or both, will be guilty of an offence and be liable to a fine of £1000 on summary conviction, or on conviction on indictment, an unlimited fine. **s4**

Records

The Secretary of State may make regulations requiring the master of any ship registered in the UK to keep records in an oil record book. Under the Oil in Navigable Waters (Records) Regulations 1972 (SI 1972 No 1929), which apply to all tankers and to ships of a gross tonnage of 80 tons or more, the information which must be entered includes the loading, transfer or discharge of oil cargo, the ballasting and cleaning of oil tanks, the disposal of oil residues and the discharge of oil bilge water. In addition, the records must contain details of any occasion on which oil or a mixture containing oil is discharged to secure the safety of a vessel, or to prevent damage to a vessel or cargo, or to save life, and any occasion on which oil or a mixture containing oil is found to have escaped or be escaping from the ship as the result of a leakage.

The Secretary of State has also made the Oil in Navigable Waters (Transfer Records) Regulations 1957 (SI 1957 No 358) which relate to the transfer of oil to and from vessels while they are in UK territorial waters. These apply to all vessels, registered or not, of whatever nationality, and which either are capable of carrying in bulk over 25 tons of oil or are constructed or fitted to carry in bulk over 5 tons of oil in one space or container, in either case for cargo or bunker purposes.

Records must contain information on matters such as the name and port of registry, if any, of the vessel, the date, time and place of the transfer, the amount and description of oil transferred, and from which vessel, barge or place to which vessel, barge or place it was transferred.

In the case of a transfer of oil to a barge, the records are to be kept by the person supplying the oil; in the case of a transfer from a barge, the records are to be kept by the person receiving the oil.

Failure to keep these records is an offence, and the owner or master, or both, will be liable to a maximum penalty on summary conviction of £500. Knowingly to make a statement in a record which is false or misleading in a material particular is an offence with a maximum penalty on summary conviction of a fine of £500, or six months' imprisonment, or both, and on conviction on indictment, an unlimited fine, or two years' imprisonment, or both. s17

Notification

If any oil or mixture containing oil is discharged into the waters of a harbour in the UK from a vessel, or is found to be escaping or to have escaped from a vessel into these waters, or is found to be escaping or to have escaped into them from a place on land, the owner or master of the vessel, or the occupier of the place, must report this forthwith to the harbour master or, if there is none, to the harbour authority. The report must specify whether it is a discharge or an escape.

Failure to make a report is a criminal offence with a maximum penalty on summary conviction of £200. **s11**

Restrictions on transfer of oil at night

No oil is to be transferred to or from a vessel between sunset and sunrise in any harbour in the UK unless notice has been given, or it is for the purpose of a fire brigade. Notice must be given to the harbour master, or if there is none, to the harbour authority. A general notice may be given that transfers will be frequently carried out between sunset and sunrise during a specified period not exceeding twelve months. In other cases where there is no general notice, notice must be given not less than three hours and not more than ninety-six hours before the transfer.

Failure to comply with this requirement is an offence carrying a maximum penalty on summary conviction of a fine of £100. **s10**

Shipping casualties

Where an accident has occurred to or in a ship from which, in the opinion of the Secretary of State, oil may or will cause pollution on a large scale in the UK or in UK territorial waters and urgent action is necessary, he may give directions to prevent or reduce oil pollution. Such direction may be issued to the owner of the ship, or any person in possession of it, the master, or any salvor. It may require this person to take any steps whatsoever and, in particular, to move or not to move the ship, to load or not to unload any oil or other cargo, or to take specified salvage measures. If the Secretary of State is of the opinion that the power to issue directions is inadequate, he may take action of any kind whatsoever, including taking control of the ship and sinking or destroying it or its cargo.

Contravening or failing to comply with a direction is an offence unless the accused can prove that he used all due diligence to comply, or had reasonable cause to believe that compliance would have involved serious risk to human life.

It is an offence to obstruct anyone acting on the Secretary of State's behalf in serving a direction, acting in pursuance of the direction, or acting under the powers given to the Secretary of State.

The maximum penalties which can be imposed for these offences are, on summary conviction, a fine of £50000, and on conviction on indictment, an unlimited fine.

If action is taken in pursuance of a direction or under the Secretary of State's powers and it was not reasonably necessary to prevent or reduce oil pollution, or the good it did or was likely to do was disproportionately less than the expense incurred or damage suffered as the result of the action, a person suffering loss or damage is entitled to compensation from the Secretary of State. When deciding whether there is a right to compensation, account must be taken of the extent and risk of oil pollution had the action not been taken, the likelihood of the action being effective, and the extent of the damage caused by the action. **s12–14**

Enforcement

Inspectors

The Secretary of State may appoint inspectors to report to him whether the provisions of the Act are being complied with, and what measures have been taken to prevent the escape of oil and mixtures containing oil.

Inspectors have power to board vessels and test equipment, to require the production of any records or books, and to copy records in order to enforce the Act. **s18**

Legal proceedings

Proceedings for an offence under the Act may only be brought by or with the consent of the Attorney General and, in some circumstances, by harbour authorities, the Secretary of State or a person authorised by him. Only the Director of Public Prosecutions can prosecute under s3.

Where an offence under s3 is committed by a body corporate with the consent or connivance of, or was attributable to the neglect of, any director, secretary, manager or other officer, he, as well as the body corporate, is liable to be proceeded against and punished. **s19**

Oil Pollution at Sea: Civil Liability

The Merchant Shipping (Oil Pollution) Act 1971

Liability

Where, as the result of any occurrence while a ship is carrying a cargo of persistent oil in bulk, any of the oil carried, either as part of cargo or otherwise, is discharged or escapes from the ship, the owner, unless an exemption applies, will be liable for:

(a) Any damage caused in the area of the UK by contamination resulting from the discharge or escape, ie, on land, in inland waters, or within territorial waters.
(b) The cost of any measures taken to prevent or reduce the consequences of such a discharge or escape.
(c) Any damage caused as the result of such remedial measures.

However, the owner will not incur liability if he proves that the discharge or escape resulted from an act of war or hostilities, or from an exceptional, inevitable and irresistible natural phenomenon, or was due wholly to anything done or not done by a person, not being his servant or agent, with intent to do damage, or was due to the default of a government or other authority in maintaining any navigational aids.

No servant or agent of the owner will be liable under the above, nor will any person performing salvage operations with the agreement of the owner. **ss1, 2, 3**

Limitation of liability

Where an owner of a ship incurs liability under the above by reason of a discharge or escape which occurred without his actual fault or privity, the limitation of liability provisions of the Merchant Shipping Act 1894 do not apply, but the Act itself contains provisions for such a limitation. He may limit his liability to 2000 gold francs for each ton of the ship's tonnage, or 210 million gold francs, whichever is the smaller. Under the Merchant Shipping (Sterling Equivalents) (Various Enactments) (No 2) Order 1978 (SI 1978 No 1468) these amounts are £86.83 and £9 117 024 respectively.

Where the court decides that a person is entitled to limit his liability, it must, after directing payment into court, ascertain the amount which would be payable to the persons making claims without considering any limitation, and then divide the amount paid into court among those persons in proportion to their claims. **ss4–8**

Compulsory insurance

Any ship carrying in bulk more than 2000 tons of persistent oil must not enter or leave a port in the UK, or arrive at or leave a terminal in UK territorial waters, nor, if it is a ship registered in the UK, enter or leave a port in another country, or arrive at or leave a terminal in the territorial sea of another country, unless there is a current certificate of insurance or other security covering the owner's liability.

Contravention of this provision is an offence carrying a maximum penalty on summary conviction of £35 000, and on conviction on indictment, an unlimited fine.

In respect of UK registered ships, such a certificate must be issued by the Secretary of State if he is satisfied that such insurance or other security will be in force. If there is a doubt as to whether the person providing this will be able to meet his obligations, or whether the insurance or security covers all the relevant liability, he may refuse to issue a certificate.

The Oil Pollution (Compulsory Insurance) Regulations 1977 (SI 1977 No 85) contain details of the procedure to be followed and also include the definition of persistent oil, which is basically hydrocarbon mineral oils, residual oils from refining or distilling, and whale oil. **ss10, 11**

The Merchant Shipping Act 1974

This Act implements an international convention on the establishment of an international fund for compensation for oil pollution damage.

Under the 1971 Act, a person who has suffered damage as the result of oil pollution may, nevertheless, fail to obtain compensation. This convention and the Act are designed to provide a remedy in such a situation.

Compensation fund

Contributions are to be payable to the fund in respect of oil carried by sea to ports or terminals in the UK, whether or not the oil is being imported, and whether or not contributions have been paid in respect of the carriage of the same oil on a previous voyage.

Contributions are also payable in respect of oil received at any installation in the UK after having been discharged in a country not party to the convention. The person liable to pay the contribution is the importer in the case of oil imported into this country, and in any other case the person who receives the oil. A person will not be liable for contributions in respect of a year if in that year he receives or imports less than 150 000 tonnes of oil.

175

To ascertain the names of persons liable to contribute to the fund, and the amount of oil for which they are liable, the Secretary of State may require, by notice, anyone engaged in producing, treating, distributing or transporting oil to furnish such information as may be specified.

Failure to comply with this notice, or deliberately or recklessly to make a statement false in a material particular is a criminal offence punishable on summary conviction with a maximum of a £400 fine, and on conviction on indictment, an unlimited fine, or up to twelve months' imprisonment, or both.

Disclosure of information obtained by such a notice is an offence punishable on summary conviction with a maximum fine of £400, unless the disclosure was made with the consent of the person who made it, was in connection with the execution of this provision, or was for the purpose of legal proceedings arising out of this provision, or a report of such proceedings. **ss1–3**

Claims for Compensation

A person who suffers damage as a result of oil pollution has a claim on the fund if he has not been able to obtain full compensation under s1 of the Merchant Shipping (Oil Pollution) Act for any of the following reasons:

(a) That the discharge or escape causing the damage was:
   (i) caused by an exceptional, inevitable and irresistible phenomenon;
   (ii) due wholly to anything done or not done by another person, not being the servant or agent of the owner, with intent to do damage;
   (iii) due to the neglect or default of a government or other authority in maintaining any navigational aids;
   so as to exclude liability under s2 of the 1971 Act.
(b) Because the owner or guarantor liable for the damage cannot meet his obligations in full. This arises when the obligations have not been met after all reasonable steps to pursue the available legal remedies have been taken.
(c) Because the damage suffered exceeds the liability as limited under the provisions relating to limitation of liability.

The fund will not be liable if the pollution damage resulted from an act of war, hostilities, etc, or was caused by oil from a warship or other ship used wholly on governmental non-commercial service. It will not be liable if the claimant cannot prove that the damage

176

resulted from an occurrence involving a ship identified by him, or involving two or more ships, one of which was identified by him.

The fund may be excused either wholly or partly from its obligations if the damage resulted wholly or partly from an act or omission on the part of the person who suffered the damage with intent to do damage, or from his negligence.

The fund must indemnify the owner of a ship and his guarantor for that portion of liability under s1 of the 1971 Act which is in excess of 1500 gold francs per ton of the ship's tonnage, or a total of 125 million gold francs, whichever is the less, and which is less than 2000 gold francs per ton or 210 million gold francs, whichever is the less. **ss4, 5**

Tankers

This Act gives the Secretary of State powers to make rules prescribing requirements to be complied with by UK oil tankers in respect of their design and construction. It also contains restrictions on tankers sailing from ports unless certain requirements are complied with.

Town and Country Planning

In a work of this nature, a detailed discussion of town and country planning legislation would be out of place. However, some provisions are of particular relevance to problems of waste and pollution.

The major piece of legislation is the Town and Country Planning Act 1971. The local planning authorities responsible for enforcing the Act are county councils and district councils. Two aspects of planning legislation need to be examined, development plans and development control.

Development Plans

A county council is normally responsible for preparing a structure plan, the strategic planning document for the area of the authority.

The area must be surveyed to examine matters which may be expected to affect the development of the area or the planning of its development. In particular, the survey must cover the principal physical and economic characteristics of the area, the size, composition and distribution of the population, communications and transport, and any other relevant matters.

The authority must then prepare a draft structure plan which is a written statement formulating its policy and general proposals in respect of the development and other land use in the area, including measures for the improvement of the physical environment and the management of traffic. In addition, the plan must contain appropriate diagrams, illustrations and other descriptive matter.

The results of the survey and the draft plan must be publicised to give members of the public an opportunity to make representations. The structure plan must be approved by the Secretary of State.

Local plans must also be prepared where appropriate. These are normally undertaken by district councils, and are to supplement the structure plan. Proposals in them must broadly conform to the strategy contained in the structure plan. The proposals must be publicised, but normally the Secretary of State does not have to approve them.

In addition, where a structure plan contains proposals for an action area, ie, an area selected for comprehensive treatment during a specified period by development, redevelopment or improvement, a local plan containing details of the action proposed must be prepared. Local plans may be prepared on a subject basis to enable detailed consideration to be given to particular problems.

These give a framework within which the area of a local authority can change and thus include matters affecting the problems of waste and pollution control—in particular, measures for the improvement of the physical environment. For instance, plans which define a disposal authority's intentions regarding waste and its disposal will have to take account of the overall planning strategy contained in the structure plan.

Development Control

The most important aspect of town and country planning legislation is that development will only be allowed if planning permission has been obtained. The definition of development in this context is the carrying out of building, engineering, mining or other operations, in, over or under land, or the making of any material change of use of any buildings or other land.

This definition falls into two parts: (i) operations which essentially involve the physical alteration of the land and (ii) change of use, which is concerned with the use to which existing buildings and land are put. Building, mining and quarrying come in the first category, but matters such as changing a shop into a factory, or a quarry into a waste tip, would fall into the second.

Obviously, a new waste tip is development since it involves a change of use, but the Act extends the definition of development in the case of refuse tips. The deposit of refuse or waste materials on land involves a material change of use, even though the land is part of a site already used for that purpose, if the superficial area of the deposit is extended or its height increases to exceed the level of the land adjoining the site. Thus, in certain circumstances, to continue tipping once a pit is full will constitute development for which planning permission is required.

Once it is established that there will be development as defined above, it can only proceed if planning permission is obtained, unless it is an exception for which planning permission is not necessary. **ss22, 23**

Applications for planning permission

Application must be made to the relevant planning authority, usually the district council. An application is not normally publicised except where the Secretary of State so prescribes.

Cases where applications must be publicised contained in the General Development Order 1977 (SI 1977 No 289) include:

(a) The construction of buildings or other operations or the use of land for the disposal of refuse or waste materials, or as a scrap yard, or for mineral workings.

(b) The construction of buildings or other operations or the use of land for the retention, treatment or disposal of sewage, trade waste or sludge.

Notice of such an application must be published in a local paper, and also affixed to the land in question. Any member of the public has a right to make representations to the local planning authority within twenty-one days of such publication. Before determining the application the authority must consider these representations.

Any application to which the above requirements apply must be accompanied by a copy of the notice, evidence that it has been published, and a certificate stating either that the notice has been affixed on the land in question, or that the applicant was unable to affix it because he did not have right of access or other rights which would have permitted him to do so, and that although he took reasonable steps to acquire them he was unable to do so. **s26**

In certain cases the local authority must consult specified bodies. In particular, the relevant water authority must be consulted where the development consists of or includes:

(a) The carrying out of works or operations in the beds of or on the banks of a river or a stream.
(b) The carrying out of building, or other operations or use of land for the purpose of refining or storing mineral oils and their derivatives.
(c) The use of land for the deposit of any kind of refuse or waste.
(d) The carrying out of building or other operations on land, or the use of land for the retention, treatment or disposal of sewage, trade waste or sludge.

Grant of planning permission

The local planning authority may grant permission either unconditionally or subject to conditions, or may refuse to grant it. The decision must be notified within two months of the application, or such longer period as may be agreed.

A person who has been refused permission or has been granted it conditionally, or to whom no decision has been notified within the time limit, may appeal to the Secretary of State.

The Act states that the authority may impose such conditions as it thinks fit when granting planning permission. In particular, conditions may be imposed to regulate the development of the land or its use, or to require the carrying out of works expedient for the purposes of or in connection with the authorised development. They may also require the removal of buildings or the discontinuance of a use at the end of a specified period, and works to be carried out to reinstate the land at the end of that time.

However, an authority does not have a totally unfettered discretion. Conditions must be for some planning purpose, and must not be unreasonable, uncertain or ambiguous. Subject to such restrictions, conditions may be imposed to minimise the effect of the development of the area. For example, they may be imposed to regulate noise, smells or smoke, although it should be noted that a planning permission does not of itself constitute a defence under, for instance, the Clean Air Acts.

Planning permission may be granted for the use of a site as a refuse tip. A condition normally imposed is that any tipping must be carried out with the authority of and in accordance with the terms of the disposal licence granted by the disposal authority. **ss29, 30**

180

Enforcement

Some system of enforcement is needed where development takes place without planning permission, and where conditions attached to planning permission are not observed.

In outline only, the procedure is as follows. If the authority is of the opinion that there is an unpermitted development or a breach of conditions, it may serve an enforcement notice specifying the breach of planning control, the steps to be taken to remedy it, the date when the notice takes effect and the period within which it must be complied with. Where the breach is the carrying out of operations without permission or a breach of a condition attached to a planning permission, an enforcement notice must be served within four years of the breach.

Failure to comply with an enforcement notice is a criminal offence. In addition, where the enforcement notice specifies work to be carried out, the authority may, in the event of a default, enter on the land, carry out the works and recover the costs from the person in default.

It is possible to appeal against an enforcement notice to the Secretary of State. Where there is an appeal, the effect of the enforcement notice is suspended pending the determination of the appeal.

To be valid, an enforcement notice must be clear and unambiguous so that the person on whom it is served may ascertain exactly what he must do in order to comply. If it is not, it will be a nullity and of no legal effect; see, for example, the case of Metallic Protectives Ltd v Secretary of State for the Environment. An enforcement notice was served alleging that there had been a breach of a condition that no nuisance should be caused to residential properties by noise, smells, etc. The company was required to install satisfactory soundproofing on a compressor, and to minimise the effects of using acrylic paint. It was held by the Divisional Court that the notice was too vague and imprecise to be amended by the Secretary of State, and was invalid and a complete nullity. **ss87, 88, 89**

As has been mentioned, if there is an appeal against an enforcement notice, the effect of the notice is suspended pending the determination of the appeal, and the alleged breach of planning control will be permitted to continue during that period. However, in respect of operations (though not a change of use) which are an alleged breach of planning control, a local authority may serve a stop notice when there is an appeal against an enforcement notice.

A stop notice requires specified operations to cease during the period until the appeal against the enforcement notice is determined. However, if the enforcement notice is subsequently quashed or withdrawn, the local authority will be liable to pay compensation. For the purpose of this provision only, the deposit of refuse or waste materials on land where that constitutes a breach of planning control will come within the definition of operations and thereby be subject to the stop notice procedure. **s90**

Radioactive Materials

It is not proposed to deal in detail with this topic, but merely to indicate some of the more important provisions of the legislation, in particular the Radioactive Substances Act 1960.

Registration

Unless registered with the Secretary of State or exempt from registration, no one is permitted to keep on any premises or to permit or cause to be kept on any premises any radioactive material, nor is anyone permitted to use, let or hire any mobile radioactive apparatus.

In either case the registration can be subject to such conditions and qualifications as the Secretary of State thinks fit.

Accumulation and Disposal of Radioactive Waste

Without an authorisation from the Secretary of State, no person is allowed to accumulate on any premises used for an undertaking carried on by him any radioactive waste with a view to its subsequent disposal. This authorisation may be granted subject to conditions or otherwise qualified.

Anyone who wishes to dispose of radioactive waste on or from premises he occupies for the purpose of an undertaking or from mobile radioactive apparatus must have a prior authorisation from the Secretary of State.

Also, a person who receives any radioactive waste for the purpose of disposal by him must not dispose of it except in accordance with an authorisation granted by the Secretary of State. Any authorisation for the disposal of radioactive waste may be given subject to conditions.

Where there is in force an authorisation to dispose of waste, it is not necessary to obtain an authorisation to accumulate the waste, as the former extends to both operations.

Transport of Radioactive Waste

Under the Radioactive Substances Act 1948, the Secretary of State has powers to make regulations concerning the use, treatment, etc, and transport of radioactive substances. The regulations in force are the Radioactive Substances (Carriage by Road) (Great Britain) Regulations 1974 (SI 1974 No 1735), and the Radioactive Substances (Road Transport Workers) (Great Britain) Regulations 1970 (SI 1970 No 1827) as amended by the Radioactive Substances (Road Transport Workers) (Great Britain) (Amendment) Regulations 1975 (SI 1975 No 1522).

Motor Vehicles

Under the Motor Vehicles (Construction and Use) Regulations 1978 (SI 1978 No 1017) there are controls on the use of motor vehicles, designed to prevent air pollution and excessive noise. There are also detailed requirements relating to motor vehicle construction to minimise the emission of atmospheric pollutants and noise. Reference should be made to the regulations for details.

Regulations to Prohibit or Restrict the Import and Use, etc, of Injurious Substances

Under the Control of Pollution Act, the Secretary of State may, if he considers it appropriate, make regulations to prohibit or restrict the import, the landing and unloading in the UK, the use in connection with any trade, business or manufacturing process, or the supply for any purpose of any specified substances so as to prevent them from causing damage to persons, animals or plants, or the pollution of air, water or land. Contravention of these regulations is an offence carrying a maximum penalty of a fine of £400 on summary conviction, and on conviction on indictment, two years' imprisonment, or an unlimited fine, or both.

Before making such regulations, the Secretary of State must consult the representatives of persons likely to be affected, and publish in the London Gazette and any other appropriate publication a notice indicating the effect of the proposed regulations, and stating that representations concerning them may be made to him. **s100**

APPLICATION TO SCOTLAND

The main text is concerned with the law of pollution control as it applies in England and Wales. The purpose of this appendix is to outline the law as it applies in Scotland, but in the space available it is only possible to indicate the main effects of the legislation. It should be noted that, although legislation may apply both to Scotland and to England and Wales, often the dates on which the various provisions come into force are different.

Local Authorities

The system of local government in Scotland is different from that in England and Wales. The Western Isles, the Orkneys and the Shetlands each have an Islands Council. The rest of Scotland is divided into regions which are in turn divided into districts. Although in some respects this division corresponds with the division in England and Wales into counties and districts, the comparison is far from exact.

Common Law

Remedies equivalent to an injunction and damages may be obtained in the Scottish courts, and in general terms the torts of negligence, nuisance and the Rule in Rylands v Fletcher involve liability on principles similar to those of English law.

Pollution of Inland Waters

The authorities responsible for the enforcement of the legislation relating to inland water pollution are the River Purification Boards. Under the Rivers (Prevention of Pollution) (Scotland) Acts 1951 and 1965 there is a system of consents similar to that under the Rivers (Prevention of Pollution) Acts 1951 and 1961 in England and Wales. When they are eventually brought into force, most of the relevant provisions of the Control of Pollution Act will be applicable in Scotland.

In Scotland, local authorities remain responsible for sewage disposal, including trade effluents. Under the Sewerage (Scotland) Act 1968 there is a system of consents to discharge of trade effluent similar to that in England and Wales under the trade effluent legislation.

Waste on Land

The relevant provisions of the Control of Pollution Act 1974 apply in Scotland and the position is broadly the same as in England and Wales. In Scotland, however, Islands and District Councils have the responsibilities of both collection and disposal authorities.

Control of Noise

The relevant provisions of the Control of Pollution Act 1974 apply in Scotland and are enforced by Islands and District Councils.

Air Pollution

The Alkali Act and the Health and Safety at Work Act apply in Scotland.

The Clean Air Acts and the relevant parts of the Control of Pollution Act apply in Scotland and are enforced by Islands and District Councils.

186

Enforcement

The enforcement powers of the Control of Pollution Act are conferred on 'relevant authorities'; in Scotland these are the Secretary
of State, River Purification Boards and Islands and District Councils.

Where in England and Wales there is a right of appeal to a
magistrate's court, in Scotland there is a right of appeal to a sheriff.

As a general rule in Scotland, only the procurator-fiscal may
bring criminal proceedings; bodies such as River Purification Boards
may not bring prosecutions under the various statutes in the same
way as may, for example, English regional water authorities.

FURTHER READING

Legal Aspects of Pollution Control

Tort

Reference may be made to any standard legal textbook, such as the following (all published by Sweet and Maxwell):

Clerk and Lindsell, *Law of Torts*
Salmond, *Law of Torts*
Winfield and Jolowicz, *Tort*

Pollution Control

The Control of Pollution Encyclopaedia, edited by J.F. Garner (Butterworth, 1977), contains the annotated texts of the Statutes and Statutory Instruments together with various precedent forms.

The Law and Practice Relating to Pollution Control in the United Kingdom, by J. McLoughlin, (Graham and Trotman, 1977), is one of a series of works dealing with the law on pollution control in the member countries of the EEC.

Wider Aspects of Pollution Control

Useful works of reference include:

Various HMSO publications, particularly the series *Pollution Papers* and *Waste Management Papers*, which contain information on pollution and waste in general, and also on specific topics.

Directory of Waste Disposal and Recovery, edited by Alan Pratt for the Chemical Recovery Association (George Godwin, 1978), which gives details of public bodies, companies, etc, concerned with waste disposal and pollution control, together with useful articles on technical and legal aspects of the subject.

Waste Recycling and Pollution Control Handbook, by A.J. Bridgwater and C.J. Mumford (George Godwin, 1979), which gives information on the practical aspects of pollution control and contains an extensive bibliography as well as details of disposal and recovery operations and much tabulated data.

INDEX

194